Practitioner Research at Doctoral Level

In trying to juggle the various priorities of doctoral study, many individuals struggle. From gathering data, preparing papers and organising projects, to the less obvious difficulties of time management and personal development, doctoral researchers are heavily tasked. In addition to this, those undertaking practitioner research face the complication of negotiating a less traditional research setting.

As a guide to this ongoing, often neglected aspect of doctoral research, the authors of this innovative book explore in detail the challenges faced by doctoral researchers conducting practitioner research today. They show that the special nature of this research and the conditions in which the professional researcher works raise questions about producing new knowledge at work through research and the ways power plays through the process. This affects everything: relationships with practice; ethics; the ways that they are taught and supervised; the genre of the thesis; all place practitioners in situations which may not methodologically align with conventional approaches.

In this book the authors take the opportunity to explore these themes in an holistic and integrated way in order to develop a sense of methodological coherence for the practitioner researcher at doctoral level. In doing so, the authors argue for what is possible, suggesting that universities should critically examine practitioner doctorates to accommodate new forms of knowledge formation.

As an invaluable guide through doctoral research, this book will be essential reading for both doctoral researchers and supervisors alike, as well as practitioner researchers working in professional settings more generally and those engaging in policy debates about doctoral research.

Pat Drake is Senior Lecturer in Education at the University of Sussex, UK.

Linda Heath is Senior Lecturer in the Business School at the University of Brighton, UK.

Practitioner Research at

D

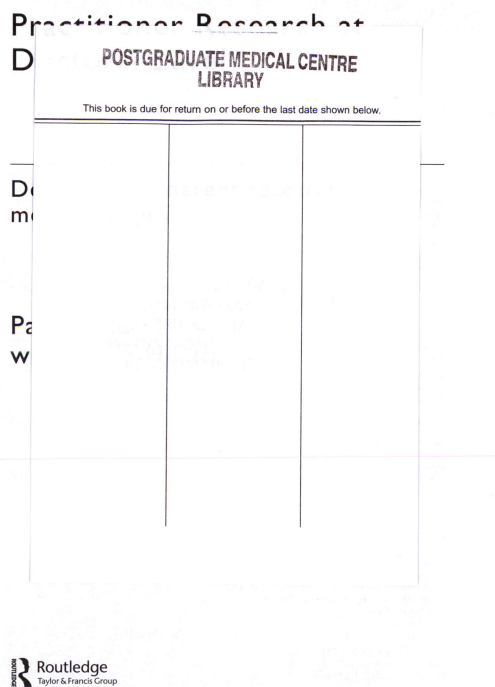

D

m

Pa

w

Routledge
Taylor & Francis Group

LONDON AND NEW YORK

First edition published 2011
by Routledge
2 Park Square, Milton Park, Abingdon, Oxon OX14 4RN

Simultaneously published in the USA and Canada
by Routledge
270 Madison Avenue, New York, NY 10016

Routledge is an imprint of the Taylor & Francis Group, an informa business

© 2011 Pat Drake and Linda Heath

The right of Pat Drake and Linda Heath to be identified as
authors of this work has been asserted by them in accordance
with sections 77 and 78 of the Copyright, Designs and Patents
Act 1988.

Typeset in Galliard by Wearset Ltd, Boldon, Tyne and Wear
Printed and bound in Great Britain by TJ International Ltd,
Padstow, Cornwall

British Library Cataloguing in Publication Data
A catalogue record for this book is available from the British Library

Library of Congress Cataloging-in-Publication Data
Drake, Pat.
Practitioner research at doctoral level : developing coherent
research methodologies / Pat Drake with Linda Heath.
p. cm.
1. Doctoral students. 2. Dissertations, Academic–Research–
Methodology. I. Heath, Linda, 1949- II. Title.
LB2386.D73 2011
001.4'2–dc22

2010015841

ISBN13: 978-0-415-49021-4 (hbk)
ISBN13: 978-0-415-49022-1 (pbk)
ISBN13: 978-0-203-84100-6 (ebk)

For Kitty

Contents

Illustrations

Figure

Tables

Acknowledgements

We are grateful to the following for sharing their ideas: Sarah Aynsley, Marcia Behrenbruch, Lorraine Beveridge, John Crossland, Barbara Crossouard, Karen Felstead, Louise Gazeley, Fran Hunt; and to Paul Webster for his critical engagement with Chapter 5. We would also like to thank all of those people undertaking professional doctorates who found time to participate in our studies; the anonymous reviewers whose thoughtful observations helped shape the book; and particularly friends and colleagues, Liz Dunn, Mary Harris and Elaine Sharland, whose support was invaluable when the going got tough.

We are grateful for the following permission:

For drawing in Chapter 3 on pp. 128–129 from Drake, P. & Heath, L. (2008) Insider researchers in schools and universities: the case of the professional doctorate. In P. Sikes & T. Potts (eds), *Researching education from the inside: Investigating institutions from within*. London: Routledge, 127–143.

To include, in Chapter 4, Table 4.1 from p. 155 in Leonard, D. (2001) *A woman's guide to doctoral studies*. Buckingham: Open University Press.

Chapter 1

Introduction

If you are reading this book you are probably a doctoral researcher, or you might be a doctoral supervisor. Quite probably you will be engaging with insider research that complements your professional life as a practitioner in the public sectors of education, social work and health studies. You may be a candidate for a professional doctorate such as the Education Doctorate, the Doctorate of Health and Social Care or the Doctor of Business Administration. You may be on a traditional PhD programme, or undertaking one of the new PhDs that closely resemble many professional doctorates, as a practitioner researcher, working at doctoral level. You may be at the beginning of your doctoral journey, or you may have come to understand, from your experience to date, that conducting research as an insider brings its own challenges and you may be addressing these. You may not be in the same country as the university in which you are registered, and you may be undertaking your doctoral study at a distance.

Insider research depends upon the researcher having some experience or insight into the worlds in which the research is being undertaken and this may be from a personal point of view as well as, or instead of, from a professional perspective. Whilst recognising that personal values are significant, and that many of the tensions elaborated throughout the book will be experienced also by those who are not engaged as professionals in the research field, this book is written with a focus on practitioner research by professionals seeking a doctoral degree. As has been pointed out by others (Merton & Storer, 1973), even though insider research undertaken by practitioners often means enquiring about one's own work organisation, it is not a necessary condition. Rather, an insider researcher may be described as an individual who possesses intimate knowledge of 'the community and its members' (Hellawell, 2006: 483), and since the word 'community' has wider implications than a single organisation, possessing intimate professional knowledge does not necessarily mean being employed by a particular organisation.

The book is intended for all professionals working at doctoral level and researching practice, and for the doctoral teachers working with them. As doctoral education is undergoing a root-and-branch revision in the UK and elsewhere, some readers will also be engaging with policy debates about doctoral study.

The main objective of the book is to explore the idea that the critical position which doctoral researchers must achieve in terms of both their research and the research setting is extremely complex for practitioners conducting 'insider research'. Doctoral researchers necessarily create new knowledge. Our central proposal is that, for the insider, the newness of this knowledge comes not from a single research domain but from combining understandings from professional practice, higher education practice and the researcher's individual reflexive project. This confluence is unique for each researcher, and so new knowledge is generated in the relations between these three domains. For this to happen, the practitioner researcher maintains a fluid and flexible stance with respect to each domain, behaving sometimes as a professional, sometimes as a researcher and at all times as an author who is making meaning out of the interactions and presenting them to an external audience. This can result in nearly impossible tensions, for example, relationships with colleagues may impose ethical constraints on how to analyse research data gathered from the workplace. We argue that viewing practitioner research in this way generates new methodologies for insider researchers.

Doctoral theses of practitioner researchers are required to make an 'original' contribution to knowledge. Our case is that a practitioner researcher will have engaged with new knowledge at all stages of the project, from conceptualisation, through methodology, methods and empirical work, to the thesis. We suggest that new knowledge derives from all these dimensions of the study and informs all aspects under consideration at each stage, and is both directly connected to undertaking the project at all in a practice setting and unique to each researcher and their research.

Typically, debate about practitioner research at doctoral level tends to compare traditional PhDs and professional doctorates, regarding the production of academic and/or professional knowledge respectively. Such comparisons not only neglect the diversity of models of practitioner research at doctoral level, but also do not recognise that a paradigm shift has occurred and that the construction of knowledge in the social sciences is not limited to the type of doctoral programme through which it is engendered. Thus, such debates should, we believe, be consigned to history, for doctorates, be they professional or traditional, have moved on. However, researching in one's own workplace does bring special considerations which must be balanced against traditional doctoral research training. The compromises necessarily inherent in practitioner research must be argued for, and doing so makes it a complex and demanding endeavour. The risks are high, for not engaging with this argument may render the doctoral research trivial or mundane. It is a very great challenge to do such research well, but when it is done well it has a transformative effect on both the practitioner researcher and their approach to their work.

Our empirical research (Drake & Heath, 2008) into the experience of professional doctorate researchers provides some insight into dilemmas that need to be resolved for success to be achieved, and work by Sikes and Potts (2008), Campbell and Groundwater-Smith (2007) and Scott *et al.* (2004) have identified aspects of the special nature of practitioner research and the special conditions in which the practitioner doctoral researcher works. This work all indicates that questions including doctoral teaching and learning, ethical issues, relationships with colleagues, loyalty, duty and integrity place the practitioner in a situation that may not methodologically align with conventional approaches. In this book we take the opportunity to explore these themes in an holistic and integrated way so as to enable a developing sense of methodological coherence for the practitioner researcher at doctoral level.

We began this book because, having ourselves completed Doctorates in Education, we wanted to explore in more depth the dilemmas faced by practitioner researchers on doctoral degrees. Having subsequently undertaken an empirical study we realised that there was more to explore about the need for fluidity of the practitioner researcher position than could be dealt with in a single article. This book is intended to open up this discussion. We also have taken advantage of our own situation as insiders in higher education institutions to have 'conversations' with others involved in the doctoral journey; doctoral teachers and researchers and post-doctoral reflections from other people (from the UK and Australia) have all informed our thinking, either face to face or via email. Practitioner researchers have previously expressed their anxieties to us about the robustness of 'interviewing your mates' as a research method. Here we use 'conversation' unapologetically as a legitimate means for insiders to access the structures of the institutions in which they work. We quote from these conversations and all names are pseudonyms.

Participants in the original study in 2008, and in follow-up conversations in 2009, are shown in Tables 1.1 and 1.2. We are very grateful to everyone for their input, as each conversation added something interesting to the work.

In Chapter 2, 'Professional doctorates: equal but different?', we discuss the fact of researching one's own practice frequently being central to professional and academic work. Research degrees such as the professional doctorate, the 'new route' PhD and indeed many traditional

Table 1.1 Participants in 2008 study, professional doctorates

Name	Job and sector	Changed jobs	Completed
Alan	University lecturer	No	No
Colin	Senior university lecturer/practitioner	No	Yes
David	Principal university lecturer	No	No
Elizabeth	Primary freelance consultant	No	No
Florence	University lecturer	No	No
George	Primary headteacher	No	Yes
Jane	University administrator	Yes	No
Jonathan	Secondary headteacher	Yes	Yes
Louisa	University lecturer	Yes	No
Marian	University lecturer	No	No
Pam	Secondary school teacher	Yes	Yes
Sarah	Teacher/post-compulsory manager	Yes	No
Simon	Secondary school teacher	No	Yes

PhDs may provide the opportunity for experienced professionals in education, social work and social care – and related public services such as health, youth service, police and probation, community development and voluntary organisations – to work at doctoral level on problems that are of direct relevance to their own professional interests and institutional concerns. In this chapter we consider these interrelated issues, pointing to the complexity of any practitioner research at doctoral level. We consider the naming of doctoral degrees and discuss differences between them, for example, whether the professional doctorate degree differs from a traditional PhD.

Chapter 3, 'Relationship between doctoral research and professional life', develops a perspective on the question of whether practitioner, or insider, researchers can achieve any meaningful degree of critical distance

Table 1.2 Participants in 2009 conversations

Name	Job and sector	Completed	Changed jobs since completing
Mary	Primary headteacher	No, EdD	No
Anna	Deputy principal junior high school	Yes, EdD	Yes
Christine	Research fellow	Yes, DPhil	No
Jenny	Research Fellow	Yes, DPhil	Yes
Teresa	University lecturer	Yes, DPhil	Yes
Ella	University lecturer	Yes, DPhil	Yes
Margaret	University lecturer	No, PhD	No
Lizzie	Primary school teacher	No, EdD	No

from their workplace, or their colleagues, for it is the development of this critical position with respect to research and the research setting which defines doctoral level study. Rather than focus on the binary view of the practitioner researcher negotiating the roles of insider/outsider at the same time, we argue that these researchers adopt a range of complex positions in relation to people connected to their study and move through them in a much more fluid way. In order to manage these positions the doctoral researcher needs to adopt multiple integrities, not least to manage the prevailing macro and micro climates in the workplace that are pervaded by power relations.

This leads into Chapter 4, 'Approaching grounded methodology', in which we explore how tensions emerge for such researchers in reconciling their position as a researcher and as a responsible practitioner. We propose that this pitches insider researchers into a place that forces methodological consideration of researcher distance and what this means in terms of research integrity, validity and objectivity. This consideration leads to a methodology that is grounded in the study, and that is flexible enough to accommodate approaches to research that incorporate ways of knowing about practice that practitioners bring to their studies.

Ethical issues arising from occupying space as both responsible practitioner and vigilant researcher are discussed in Chapter 5, 'Thinking about ethical considerations', drawing attention to how codes of professional practice and codes of research ethics each serve different purposes and may demand different responses. We argue in Chapters 4 and 5 that methodology is grounded in practices inhabited by the practitioner researcher, and that ethical considerations are also necessarily situated in these practices. In Chapter 6, 'What does doctoral pedagogy bring to practitioner research?', and Chapter 7, 'The shaping of doctoral knowledge and supervision', we consider what the implications are of this relativism for constructing new knowledge, how this impinges on ways that doctoral pedagogy is constructed and on the part that the doctoral supervisor plays in helping practitioner researchers develop their original contribution to knowledge. We present a position that doctoral work is individualised and undertaken successfully by those practitioner researchers who are able to understand the relations between higher education practices: research, professional and pedagogic. From this stance we question the place of taught elements in the context of emerging doctoral researcher identity.

Publicity material for the practitioner research doctoral degrees is frequently couched in terms of the degree enabling participants, through research, to impact on their employing institutions. In Chapter 8, 'Impact of doctoral research and researcher identity', this claim is examined.

In exploring questions of impact, we draw upon the ideas of Engeström (2001), who argues that learning at work cannot all be anticipated, because learning in the workplace is situation-specific and under these conditions forms new knowledge, not predicted in advance. This forms a very individual scenario for practitioner doctoral researchers, in which, we argue, the notion of impact itself is problematic. We consider impact in relation to practice, to the research process, on the institutions involved and how these combine in helping to shape researcher identity.

In Chapter 9, 'Integrating academic and professional knowledge: writing the thesis', is a discussion of what is entailed in bringing the doctoral work out into a thesis. The relationship between concepts, ideas and theories and the relevance and application of these in professional settings is a central concept in both researching and writing (see, for example, Eraut, 1994) to bridge the theory–professional knowledge gap. However, this is far from straightforward.

The study, which may be ongoing in practice beyond the completion of the doctorate, and the resulting written thesis exemplify an endeavour of professional reflexion-in-action. In grappling with inherent challenges of research methodology arising out of overt personal involvement, the study also becomes a project in representation, in authenticity, in authorial and researcher voice. Acknowledging this dimension requires the author of the thesis to think carefully about the genre of their writing, of the extent to which they place themselves in the text and their authorial responsibilities as storyteller of other informants. The thesis becomes a representation of their own thoughts, even though these may be explicitly informed by the stated perspectives of others.

Chapter 9 concludes the book, and so ends with recognition that, in presenting, interpreting and analysing research reflexively, the author must take a stance on all of the predicaments and dilemmas presented throughout earlier chapters. This writing requires drawing on emotional as well as intellectual resources and working out what one thinks can be a painful and messy business as well as an intellectual one.

Chapter 2

Professional doctorates

Equal but different?

Research degrees, such as the professional doctorate, and new and indeed many traditional PhDs provide opportunities for experienced practitioners in education, social work, health and related fields to work at doctoral level on problems that are of direct relevance to their own professional interests and institutional concerns.

The professional doctorate is the most recent exemplification of accredited research development for practitioners. The name, professional doctorate, is an informal one, essentially arising from the expectation that the doctoral researcher is not undertaking research simply for its own sake, but with some specific and practice-oriented application in mind. Quite often the degree is part-time, in recognition that participants are also working professionally, and sometimes there is an expectation, even a requirement on the part of the providing university that the doctoral researcher is employed as well. Most frequently the professional doctoral programme includes some taught components, for the duration of which doctoral researchers work together in a cohort that may meet face to face, or may be connected to the university and possibly each other via some distance learning medium facilitated by the Internet. In the UK this distinguishes professional doctorates from other forms of doctoral study, although this distinction is not evident in Canada, the US or Australasia, where most, if not all, doctoral study includes some taught components.

The professional doctorate degree is equivalent in level to the traditional PhD, as doctoral researchers are required to successfully meet the same criteria, specified in the UK by the Quality Assurance Agency (QAA, 2008), namely that the degree is awarded for original research. Despite there being in the same specification advice that any taught components of the degree should not outweigh the research components, the professional doctorate is commonly understood in the UK to be the 'taught doctorate' with, sometimes, associated connotations of inferiority of level. Furthermore, as 'professional research' becomes conflated in meaning with 'practitioner research', so does the research aspect become the victim of an unfortunate and, as Saunders (2007) argues, indefensible value system that equates 'practitioner' with 'amateurish' in research terms, polarised from 'genuine' academic inquiry. The crux of the objection is that because the researcher is an insider in the organisation or community of practice that is the context for the research, it is difficult if not impossible to achieve an appropriate degree of critical distance.

This is not a view promoted in this book. We suggest that insider research at doctoral level may be particularly complex because of the relations that must be squared between the researcher as practitioner and the researcher as acolyte into the doctoral degree-awarding practices of higher education. The argument of the book is that this reconciliation pervades all aspects of undertaking research. Recognising the play between insider researcher and professional practitioner leads to and shows itself in the thesis as critical reflexivity inherent in every aspect of the research and writing process. Because these relations are critically important in the generation of new knowledge, consideration of them forms a strand of the thesis.

In this chapter we discuss the differences commonly used to differentiate between professional and traditional doctorates, and show that these are secondary to the need for the professional doctorate thesis to exemplify a sustained degree of reflexivity if it is to overcome objections of being uncritical. To develop the case, we discuss doing practitioner research at doctoral level from the perspectives of what doctoral programmes look like and what they are for; who undertakes practitioner research at doctoral level and why; what sort of new knowledge is created and how this might derive from the status and power relations in operation in the workplace and the position of the researcher in relation to these.

What are professional doctorates?

The notion of a professional doctorate is not new, and can be traced back to the mission of universities in the UK in the eighteenth century. At that time, the main concern of the university was with the development of the professions, but reforms of the nineteenth century challenged this conception and instead developed a degree based on the search for universal 'truth' through research which became the model for the Doctor of Philosophy degree (Scott et al., 2004). The first professional doctorate is said to have appeared in the USA, at Harvard in 1921, interestingly at about the same time as Gregory (1995) reports the first Doctor of Philosophy in the UK being awarded by the University of Oxford.

More recent professional doctorate developments have been led by Australian universities, and by 1994 the first candidates graduated. At the end of the 1990s in the UK it was becoming clear that a wide range of new postgraduate degrees was being developed in universities. These included, at doctoral level, professional doctorate degrees in a variety of disciplinary areas, such as education, engineering, business, clinical psychology, with, for example, the first UK professional doctorate in education being offered by the University of Bristol in 1992. Readers interested in the history and development of doctoral education in the UK are referred to the work of Bourner *et al.* (1999, 2001) who, as well as providing a summary of the development of doctoral education, have also explored, categorised and compared, searching to establish distinctions between the Doctor of Philosophy, i.e. the PhD, and the professional doctorate. They question the overall coherence of postgraduate doctoral provision, claiming lack of clarity in terms of overall understanding of the professional doctorate degree nationally and internationally. They also show that, despite the proliferation of new doctoral degrees, the status and position of the traditional PhD remains consistent and unchallenged.

Bourner *et al.* (1999) suggest that the re-emergence and growth of the professional doctorate in the UK reflects in part the pace of change in the professions, and in society more generally. The need for new, up-to-date knowledge of professional practice creates the need for new means of creating knowledge and theories, and, in the face of government dissatisfaction that 'traditional PhDs were not well matched to careers outside academia or an industrial research laboratory' (OST, 1993: 3), the development of professional doctorates may be seen as part of reshaping knowledge to include new paradigms for doctoral research (Usher, 2000). It is also possible, as Bourner *et al.* (1999) point out, that since the relative status of professions is partly based on the extent to which professionals can present themselves as rigorous practitioners of professional knowledge, the development of professional doctorates may also represent an opportunity to raise the status of specific professions as well as raising the status of individuals within organisations.

This presents problems for universities since they are under some pressure to develop more professionally relevant programmes, whilst at the same time maintaining the 'gold standard' of traditional doctoral study (Barnett, 2000).

Heath (2005) pursued this line of inquiry in a study that drilled down into education (professional) doctorates in British universities. This revealed further that, as well as the titles of these doctorates differing from each other (ten English universities chosen in an ad hoc manner offered programmes variously called: Doctor of Education, Taught Doctorate in Education, Education Doctorate and Professional Doctorate in Education), the term 'taught doctorate' characterised these degrees. Programmes range from including one taught element, such as a compulsory research methods unit, to comprising taught modules throughout the first three years of a four-year programme. This picture extends to other fields, and, of professional doctorates in health and in social care, some are now based almost entirely on assessed modules, with one UK higher education institution requiring 16 pieces of assessed work on a totally modularised course. Others are significantly research-based, with recognition from the funding council for research training that precedes a thesis.

Perhaps connected to the lack of coherence in professional doctoral provision, there is a lack of consensus regarding the status of professional doctorates. For example, some international students are sponsored to undertake a doctorate in the UK on the understanding that they will only be taking a PhD and not a professional doctorate. On the other hand, universities' (all over the world) recruiting faculty usually state that either a PhD or EdD/DSW is desirable or essential, and sometimes neither is required. This is discussed fully in Chapter 8.

Where guidance on different doctorates from professional bodies exists, it is often inconsistent with the practice of providing universities. For example, the QAA (2008) criteria for the award of doctorates explicitly mention 'those programmes which include a substantial taught element'. They assert that, in addition to generic doctoral criteria:[1] 'Professional doctorates aim to develop an individual's professional practice and to support them in producing a contribution to (professional) knowledge' (para. 46). Currently there is a tension around the notion of 'doctoralness' and 'taught degree', precisely because of the requirement for an original contribution to knowledge.

It is usual in countries outside Britain for doctoral degrees such as the PhD to consist of taught research methods units that must be successfully passed before the candidate begins their thesis. The UK is moving towards this approach, with calls for increased flexibility in doctoral provision. The so-called 'new route' comprises at least one year's research methods training followed by a three-year research project, and there are proposals (ESRC, 2009) that doctoral provision should, at institutional level, formalise a requirement that doctoral work includes research training at masters level. It is proposed that the flexibility of this model of 'one plus three' should be enhanced by extending possible combinations of research training plus thesis, so for instance 'two plus two' would be a possible model, as would 'two plus three'. There are also recommendations that part-time PhD study be opened up to more people, especially to attract those seeking a mid-career change of direction. Thus any tension between 'taught' research methods and 'original' research is becoming embedded in the PhD also.

Potentially these changes also blur distinctions between the traditional PhD and the professional doctorate, particularly the mode of study, full- or part-time and the length of time it takes to complete. The PhD has hitherto been conceptualised as full-time, although of course many people are undertaking it part-time. Professional doctorates are more frequently part-time (though practice varies). Should doctoral training move to incorporate more explicit recognition of the need for part-time routes, with more flexibility in ways of combining research training with the thesis, differences between the degrees will become even less clear. Professional doctorates are frequently advertised as being 'normally four or five years part-time', which is 'equivalent' to a minimum of two years full-time, the speediest possible registration time for a traditional PhD. Experience suggests that this is 'normally' unrealistic, with completion taking five or six years, frequently longer.

Thus the picture of professional doctorates is diverse, with little consistency between programmes in terms of nomenclature and mode of study, and little difference between professional and traditional doctorates in terms of success criteria. The characteristic component of taught elements has only been significant in the UK but not elsewhere in the English-speaking world, and is disappearing in the UK. If differences between traditional and professional doctorates are manifest in the esteem with which they are regarded, this distinction needs to be explored in terms of the nature of the knowledge that is produced.

Who undertakes practitioner research at doctoral level?

Whilst not all practitioner researchers undertake a professional doctorate, many take advantage of this route, though currently it is unclear what differentiates the professional doctorate thesis from a traditional PhD thesis in education, social work or health studies. The candidate's research project might not be very different, but their experience on the doctoral programme might. There may be differences in the choices made by those deciding to do it, i.e. does the fact of the doctorate being termed 'professional' attract a different group of doctoral researchers? Are people making decisions about the type of research (believing it to be about investigating practice), or the student experience of doctoral teaching (i.e. being in a taught group for the earlier stages), or perhaps the idea of being in a cohort affirms the potential for informal learning and mutual peer support.

Recently, the professional doctorate has become a route for doctoral training of new entrants into higher education, lecturer-practitioners employed to prepare new teachers, social workers or health-care workers. In our institutions this group is currently the single largest constituency, outnumbering practising teachers, social workers and other related professionals, and for these early-career researchers this doctoral degree provides access to the research culture in higher education with which lecturer-practitioners must also engage if they are to be professionally successful in the higher education setting.

A larger-scale study into doctoral provision across six Australian universities (Neumann, 2005) undertook a comfortably large number of interviews with research managers, supervisors and doctoral students ($n = 134$) from a range of disciplines across the sciences, the science-based professions, the humanities and social sciences, and the social science-based professions (2005: 175). The study showed that, in the first instance, some professional doctorate researchers appeared to be attracted by what they saw as an 'easier' framework and shorter thesis. This disparity in status also seemed evident to university managers; however, this perception of easiness was not confirmed by the doctoral teachers and supervisors in the study, who were reported as by and large not identifying much difference between doctoral students on either professional or traditional doctoral programmes. Candidates in this study who were towards the end of and completing doctoral work claimed that their professional doctorate research could as easily have been completed through a PhD route. Neumann sees the two awards as interchangeable, suggesting that individuals might be permitted to choose the degree that suits their purposes best. In fact, this lack of difference led her to suggest that appearing to emphasise differences between doctoral routes was a deliberate and what she called an 'expedient federal government policy of the 1990s which lacked a strong educational rationale' (2005: 185).

Professional doctorates may create an opportunity for universities to attract a wider group of people to doctoral study. This being so, it is worth considering what, if anything, distinguishes this wider population, and what is the context in which it is becoming apparent. Different authors have tried to find ways of differentiating between groups of doctoral researchers (e.g. Wellington & Sikes, 2006; Scott *et al.*, 2009; Boud & Lee, 2009), variously pointing to a range of personal motivations for undertaking a professional doctorate – desire for theory and a deeper insight into practice, frustration with practice, the influences of 'critical incidents' in the past, the attraction of a challenge – and a variety of extrinsic factors, such as reputation of the providing university and recommendations from friends or colleagues. Wellington and Sikes also report some participants in the EdD wanting to complete a doctorate in order to deal with personal feelings of previous failure, such as failing critical exams, and certainly our conversations with doctoral researchers from both professional and traditional doctoral routes would confirm that for some people, the status of the doctoral degree in itself redeems people from what they see as previous educational under-attainment.

However, personal motivation has to be considered in the wider context of pressure for individuals to acquire qualifications at higher and higher levels and for universities to encourage this trend – a trend that has become known as creeping credentialism. This combination of motivation and context is unique, even though it may also be contingent on considerations such as age, gender and ethnicity. It is important to explain how it works, because the reality of practitioner researchers' work on professional doctorates is that frequently they are insiders researching in their employing organisations, and so are subject to the prevailing mission, values and power relations within them.

We discussed this with three local professional doctorate convenors, who acted as informants on the basis of their experience in interviewing potential participants. Their views concurred with mine (Pat, also a professional doctorate convenor and external examiner) and it seems a fairly widely shared belief that the professional doctorate is chosen, both over the traditional PhD and over no doctorate at all, for three main reasons. First, because participants in the professional doctorate work together in the earlier phases with others in a cohort, there is a hopeful feeling of comradeship and mutual peer support from others 'in the same boat'. This may continue experience from a masters degree, and it may appeal to people who see the traditional PhD as potentially rather a lonely experience (although, as explained above, this is not the intention of future doctoral training). Second, the programme has a structure: normally taught modules and/or research training occur in a group with assessment arranged so that researchers progress through the programme knowing how they are getting on. Third, programme leaders believe people to be lured by the promise of a philosophy that makes a difference to practice.

However, once on the programme, the picture changes. Heath's study found that researchers' experience as participants did not match expectations on entry, and cohorts (with the exception of one institution where working and supporting each other in cohorts was mandatory and assessed) had fairly quickly disintegrated, because researchers claimed lack of time to meet up and/or an unwillingness to engage with other students' research problems when they felt they could be spending time working on their own, particularly in the thesis stage of the programmes. Our data (from the University of Sussex) also suggests that changes of cohort are quite likely, as people take different lengths of time to progress through the programme. Eraut's (2004a, 2004b) work helps theorise 'informal learning' as a crucial form of support for learning, meaning that successful learners set up and use additional learning opportunities, for example, initiating personal discussion with tutors, or friendships with other hard-working successful students. Emergent understanding of the development of academic knowledge and how this plays alongside the researchers' professional work leads to questions regarding the extent to which higher education explicitly facilitates these informal but crucial forms of support, and is clearly a challenge to programme providers. The rapid growth of social networking sites, and intense effort by universities to engage students through electronic means such as virtual learning environments, may provide alternative and developmental means of peer support that enhance rather than diminish the cohort experience through providing a distinctive environment in which informal learning can occur. Additionally we note that critical friendships between much smaller groups of participants, and between participant researchers and colleagues who have perhaps undertaken doctoral study themselves, or people further on in the programme, add to the repertoire of peer support. But it seems clear that cohorts that rely solely on face-to-face encounters are unsuccessful, especially as participants are not necessarily local, and even include some people who fly in from other countries.

What is more, whilst participants may embark on professional doctorates with the intention of making a difference to practice, on completion it appears that the research has made no noticeable changes to practice at an individual level. There are a number of reasons for this, amongst which we have identified local and national constraints imposed on practice resulting in an inability to make any lasting and significant changes. These might include decisions about resource allocation that prevent researched innovations being put into practice, or regulatory professional requirements that set parameters about what practice should include, or simply that policy decisions mean that the research is not timely.

The professional doctorate does seem rather peculiar. As well as being incoherently provided, so that, without considerable unpacking of universities' literature, potential recruits are unlikely to be able to tell one from another, the basis for the degree in terms of its benefits also seems to be flimsy when looked at carefully. In the next section we approach this from the perspective of new knowledge production, for through an analysis of this we can point to the distinctive nature of the professional doctorate and practitioner research.

The production of knowledge on a doctorate

In some professional settings, 'research' has become a seductive word, conveying as it does the use of considered and thoughtful intelligence to analyse problems and seek a means of moving forward in addressing them. In Chapter 3 we discuss this further, through examining the political context and the power relations in operation in the workplace and in universities that make it impossible for doctoral researchers to act neutrally without being positioned by the prevailing norms and values in both sites of construction of new knowledge. Further attempts to distinguish between practitioner and traditional doctorates have focused on the production of knowledge. Insider researchers often choose their project as a result of several years of experience of working with the issues. Thus they often have assumptions and ideas about what they expect to find out, and on the basis of their experience as a practitioner, they have a theoretical stance before beginning their project.

With the intention of improving practice, there is an expectation that professionals will engage with critical reflection (Schön, 1983, 1987), demonstrate experiential learning (Boud & Walker, 1990; Eraut, 1994), develop transferable skills and gain higher qualifications in order to make a significant contribution of knowledge of practice through research (Becher & Trowler, 2001; Bourner *et al.*, 2001). At the centre of the professional doctorate is the notion of critical reflection which links experiential learning with tacit knowledge (Eraut, 1994; Claxton, 1998). The recognition that knowledge production takes place outside the academy as well as inside it (Brennan, 1998) underpins this view.

For researchers on a professional doctorate programme, the relationship between concepts, ideas and theories and the relevance and application of these in professional life is central. Thus, the challenge of a professional doctorate can be seen as integrating learning and knowing at the highest academic level with the intention of bridging a theory–professional knowledge divide. However, as Leinhardt *et al.* point out, 'integrating knowledge learned in the academy with knowledge learned in practice, is neither trivial nor is it obvious how this integration should be accomplished' (1995: 11).

Knowledge creation can be conceptualised in various ways. A large literature regarding learning at work typically is based on the situated learning of Lave and Wenger (1991) and Wenger (1998), and on the acquisition of tacit knowledge through deliberative action detailed by Eraut (1994, 2004a, 2004b). Eraut has considered learning at work in several professional settings, from which he suggests that what happens when people learn at work is that their actions move from being at first deliberative and considered, to routine, leaving people free to recognise unusual situations and to think about these as specific problems that need out-of-the-ordinary consideration. Learners need other, more experienced practitioners to help with the acquisition of new skills and knowledge. Wenger proposes that occupational groups form communities of practice, communities which are always in flux as new people join and old-timers leave; and practice which is forever changing as well, for the interaction of newcomers with experienced practitioners stimulates change and development.

Bernstein's (1996, 1999) later thinking on the sociology of knowledge and identity proposed a model that delineated knowledge discourses through an appeal to orthogonal axes, horizontal and vertical. He proposed that horizontal discourse consists of everyday, oral, common-sense knowledge, and is not represented as forms of explicit knowledge in schools and universities. Horizontal discourse is local, segmental, context-dependent, tacit, often contradictory across contexts, but not within contexts. Acquisition of the discourse is likely to be through demonstration and exemplar modelling, often, but not always tacitly. On the other hand, vertical discourse is set out as a coherent, explicit knowledge structure, based on systematic principles, hierarchically organised and written in form, and likely to be produced in universities and prestigious schools.

Within vertical knowledge discourse there are different ways that knowledge is organised, or classified. So, for example, academic mathematics would be classified hierarchically, as traditionalists would tend to agree that there is some sort of order inherent in the mathematics. This hierarchical order is maintained through both the way the subject is learned, with mastery of some aspects seen as a pre-requisite for the mastery of others, and intellectual status being affirmed for those practitioners operating at the highest levels. Other forms of vertical knowledge, less hierarchical, such as humanities and social sciences, are also less strongly classified, but Bernstein explains that in these forms of knowledge there may be specialised modes of interrogation and specialised criteria for the production of texts. High status is awarded to the most prolifically published academic work, and knowledge may be created according to the interest and direction of the person undertaking the research or the study.

Bernstein questions the social logic of competence that implies that acquiring competence is a democratic process because the person gaining competence is active and creative in constructing what it means with respect to their practice. This logic, argues Bernstein, resonates with liberal progressive theories, even radicalism, especially those that dominated education in the late 1960s. The person is self-regulating; he or she takes a critical and sceptical stance with respect to hierarchical relations of the competence and its location, and, consequently, acquiring competence is emancipatory. However, Bernstein draws our attention to the observation that focusing on competence 'abstracts the individual from the analysis of distributions of power and principles of control which selectively specialise modes of acquisition and realisations' (1996: 56). This means that new knowledge is not simply acquired or developed by the individual researcher in a vacuum, but that the researcher is positioned in a complex and stratified set of social complexities of power and status that enable him or her to make knowledge claims.

Theorising the production of doctoral knowledge in this way has three significant implications. First, that professional knowledge, or knowledge at work, is not only different from knowledge produced in the university, but is unrecognisable within it. Second, that evidence of knowledge production in the university requires evidence of having engaged in the dominant mode of production, i.e. production of text. And third, that for the individual, this is not just a matter of acquiring a new set of competences, because the process by which competences are acquired are subject to distribution of power and institutional control. The continuation of the use of an academic thesis as the final assessment perpetuates the powerful function of the current discourse within the academy.

Gibbons *et al.* (1994) proposed knowledge of two main forms: Mode One, disciplinary knowledge, and Mode Two, trans-disciplinary knowledge. Disciplinary knowledge is constructed in the university, and whilst this may be used to address problems outside the university, the source of this knowledge is closed. Mode Two knowledge may be generated through practice or experience. Scott *et al.* fine tune this approach by proposing four modes of knowledge, where disciplinary knowledge is complemented by technical rational knowledge which brings scientific knowledge that 'transcends the local and the particular' (2004: 45). They argue that thinking about knowledge with respect to Mode One and Mode Two knowledge marginalises practitioner knowledge as incomplete because it is local and non-generalisable. To deal with this difficulty they add two further modes, Mode Three and Mode Four knowledge. Mode Three knowledge encompasses deliberation and reflection and because this form of knowledge is not teachable it is also unpredictable and specific to the context. Mode Four knowledge is concerned with the development of the individual through critical reflection, is positioned within the discourse of institutional power relations and may place doctoral researcher at odds with practice. This is discussed in detail in Chapter 7 in the context of the relationship between supervisors who are normally based in the providing university working with doctoral researchers on a thesis the professional basis for which they, the supervisors, may have little direct experience.

There is a danger of viewing the production of new forms of knowledge evident at the end of the thesis stage in an increasingly lengthy list. Rather we argue that insider researchers will engage with new knowledge at all stages of the project, from conceptualisation through methodology, methods and empirical work to writing the thesis. The term 'practical wisdom' (Flyvbjerg, 2001: 54) is helpful, for the Aristotelian concept of phronesis (which roughly translates as practical wisdom) goes beyond analytical knowledge (episteme) and technical knowledge (techne) and combines the two in an integrated form of knowledge. Insider or practitioner research can be seen through this perspective as phronesis, in so far as it produces new ways of knowing which combine both professional and technical knowledge with academic or analytical knowledge.

Thus, integrating academic and professional knowledge is difficult for insider doctoral researchers, for they are simultaneously part of the practice setting and part of the academy, and whilst new professional knowledge must be expressed in academic terms, it does not form part of the discourse of disciplinary knowledge of the academy. This means that researchers must transform their existing models of professional knowledge and replace them with a critical and analytic reflection on such knowledge. This critical reworking of knowledge leads the individual to 'become peer' (Maher *et al.*, 2008) in the sense of participating fully in the practices of the university knowledge production discourse.

Chapter 3

Relationship between doctoral research and professional life

Criticisms of research in education especially are legion, most particularly that as research is frequently undertaken by researchers and not by practitioners, it does not address real concerns nor does it facilitate the construction of an evidence base on which practice can develop (Hargreaves, 2007). Yet when practitioners do undertake research they must, despite starting from a position of knowledge and insight into what is important, take extra care to rebut attacks for not being sufficiently distant and therefore critical.

The relationship between the doctoral study and the professional setting raises several important issues for practitioner researchers, with the most important being the question of whether 'insiders' can achieve any meaningful degree of critical distance from their workplace or their colleagues. But it is the development of this critical position with respect to research and the research setting that defines doctoral-level study. Potentially this puts the insider in a place that requires the researcher to tread a fine line between the prevailing academic norms and values of the university with the norms and values of the workplace, for the researcher must be critical of the practices revealed through their study, whilst potentially continuing to engage with them.

Lave (1988) argues that 'situated learning' is not just learning in a location but is a socio-cultural cognitive activity positioned within the context and entirely related to it. These ideas are developed through a study of different occupational practices (of tailors, quartermasters, midwives, butchers in supermarkets, and of alcoholics) conducted with Wenger. Lave and Wenger (1991) argue that 'becoming a' requires a transformation of all the individuals involved, with mastery not located in particular individual experts but in the organisation of the occupational practice. Wenger (1998) then argues that a community of practice develops internal coherence according to the people engaging in it. Learners need access to the community of practice and this means learning the 'technology' of the practice to connect with the history of the practice and to participate in its culture. Within these communities there is a rapid flow of information and implied knowledge of what other members know. Scott *et al.* (2004) suggest that insiders are located within a shared way of looking at the world, and professionally this world would be the world of practice.

Professional doctoral researchers are negotiating learning in at least two communities of practice. These are the professional setting that the research sets out to illuminate and the higher education setting in which academic practice must be demonstrated. These researchers must successfully position themselves in a watershed that brings both of these sets of practices together, whilst recognising that the communities of practice themselves do not remain fixed and that part of this 'unfixing' is connected to the nature of new knowledge, the arrival of practitioners with new ways of working and the adaptations of practice that take place in accommodating these.

It is therefore not difficult to envisage that a professional doctorate researcher searching for an appropriate position may encounter various challenges. 'Becoming' is entirely related to where the researcher decides to position themselves.

Insider researchers often choose their project as a result of several years of experience of working with the issues. The doctoral process moves researchers from real-world observations into designing research and developing theoretical concepts to frame them. Insiders often have assumptions and ideas about what they expect to find out, and on the basis of experience as a practitioner, they may also have a theoretical stance before beginning their doctoral project. Research in the workplace is likely to be small scale involving few people. This closeness may seem to compromise the researcher's ability to critically engage with information, and so they need to devise means of stimulating reflexivity whenever possible, as an important aspect of 'self-triangulation' of their interpretations of their data. Explicitly locating oneself and one's ideas in the research project and exploring what that means for the project is an approach that leads to reflexivity.

In this chapter we explore the complexities of practitioner research, suggesting that fluidity of position is the inevitable trade-off that comes from researching things in situations that one already knows quite a lot about. Being able to take existing knowledge and build theory through research design and analytical explanation characterises successful doctoral practice.

The ways that power is distributed throughout professional settings affects both the need to do a doctoral degree, and the approaches that doctoral researchers take with respect to it. Professionals undertaking research are inextricably intertwined with their colleagues in ways that are germane to their thinking about the research project. First, colleagues on whom students are dependent for data have different and unknown personal motivations with respect to ultimately similar institutional performance ends. Second, position as a researcher is entwined with other positions in relation to people at work: maybe manager, teacher, friend and assessor. Last, as the stimulus for the research emerges from questions arising at work, it is difficult to think of ways to consider these questions without explicitly addressing the fact that there is a relationship of sorts between all the individuals connected with the issues under investigation.

One way of conceptualising research enquiry is by 'making the familiar strange' (Goodson, 1992). Doing so immediately places the practitioner researcher at a distance from the cosy 'shared understanding' that characterises professional life. To start from the premise that insiders have a shared way of looking at the world is not to understand the micro-politics of any organisation. So we offer an analysis of the way power, as conceptualised by Foucault (1977, and explained in Gutting, 1994), operates in the professional and academic setting and suggest that research activity in these settings is an instrument of power. This leads to consideration of insider-outsiderness, and what it means to inhabit the hyphen. Finally in the chapter, we apply these ideas to relationships with colleagues and what it means to become a practitioner researcher.

Power and professional settings

People at work in education institutions of all kinds operate in intensely political climates. Dominant ideologies allow for little dissent, and create practices through the distribution of power between people in the organisation and through dominant sets of relations regarding practice. It is quite impossible for people operating in these regimes to ignore the dominant practices, quite impossible, for example, for a teacher to teach in a state school without paying attention to the national curriculum or to the governmental means of assuring it (in the UK this is the Office for Standards in Education, Ofsted). Nor would it be possible for a social worker to disregard expectations that he or she adhere to the code of practice set out by the General Social Care Council (in the UK) or for a registered health practitioner to prescribe unorthodox forms of treatment.

Whilst there are differences between individuals in professional settings in terms of power and status within the organisation, ultimately most behave as what Foucault calls 'docile subjects' and become conditioned to behave and even think in ways that are in the interests of the prevailing paradigms. To establish the new forms of social control, individuals, suggests Foucault, need to be re-trained and re-disciplined to accept the new constraints.

Even though we frequently inhabit multiple positions – for example, our public professional position may differ from privately expressed views – the ways that we manoeuvre are contingent on who we are and how others perceive us. Moreover, this is a unique combination, even though these perceptions may also be contingent on considerations such as age, gender, ethnicity and class.

Foucault argued that power and knowledge are interactively and dynamically connected and, thus, not possessed by an individual or an institution independently, but everywhere distributed through complex social networks. Thus, for a dominant agent to achieve control there must be power relations with peripheral agents to establish or reinforce connections between dominance and the fulfilment of subordinates' desires. That is to say, people in the institution must be personally desirous of knowing or achieving something that only that institution or others in it can provide, and there must be a knowledge exchange. Thus, institutional policies are implemented through facilitating these desired experiences.

In contemporary professional settings such as in education, social work or health, performance is crucial, and is monitored in various ways. Foucault called the process of policing institutions to ensure docility on the part of the subjects within them 'surveillance', and it is a means through which regulation of social institutions is achieved; consider, for example, the proliferation of examinations in military, hospital, medical, scholastic or employment interviews. Two additional components also aid regulation. These are confession/elicitation and documentation. Each of the three elements – surveillance, confession and documentation – provides knowledge about individuals within the system. Indeed, each of these forms of control as techniques for enhancing productivity in the public services have proliferated hugely, with explicit tensions emerging between the instrumentalism of government, on the one hand, and traditional liberalism, on the other.

Foucault also pointed to the massive but infrequent exercise of destructive force (he suggested, by way of example, public executions, military occupations) that demonstrates unequivocally where power lies. We can apply this idea to educational, social service or health settings, and note that an example of a 'destructive force' might be the withdrawal of funding from an institution for 'non-compliance' with an imposed set of regulatory procedures, or 'naming and shaming' those institutions that comply less successfully with prevailing regulations.

Power, according to Foucault, becomes more dominant when one has information not only about what subjects do, but also about how and why they come to think and believe as they do. In educational or public service institutions, surveillance is achieved not just on the macro level of checking institutional outputs against externally derived criteria, but also through documentation and confession/elicitation. In the absence of sufficient funding, the collective pursuit of more resources depends upon the will of individual employees being aligned towards this goal (which can only be achieved when the institution is recognised as being 'deserving' through its excellence with respect to these dominant criteria). Thus, docility of the institution depends upon the obedience of its staff who must all be persuaded that it is in their interests to work towards common goals. Gramsci's (1971) concept of hegemony is helpful in understanding how this works. Gramsci probes at questions of the moral authority by which leading groups are accepted as having the power to influence other groups. Thus, for example in higher education, the need to publish, to teach, to increase research activity and to generate more students in ever diverse ways is accepted because the discourse is hegemonic – what it means to be a successful academic is transformed into synonymy which has to be monitored. This monitoring or policing is achieved largely through scrutiny of texts (online or on paper). The entire modus operandi of universities with respect to their students is through scrutiny of texts in the shape of essays or responses to examination questions, and especially through assessment of research projects of doctoral students, who are required to contribute to the overall knowledge-producing effort through the contribution of an original thesis.

The doctoral research process in a professional setting can be seen as eliciting just such evidence from the professional setting, and the production of the thesis is a further stage in the transformation of this professional evidence into an academic discourse.

Thus the practitioner researcher is positioned not only by the prevailing power relations in the professional setting but also, in the case of practitioner doctoral students, by the prevailing ideologies of knowledge production in the university as well. Both of these sets of forces combine to ensure that the research is neither objective nor neutral, and the methodological approach will necessarily take account of the need for the researcher to navigate these very tricky, and fluid, boundaries.

Insider researchers are members of an organisation or practice with a particular culture, ethos and workplace mission. In researching the one's own workplace, one is inevitably positioned by the prevailing political ideologies, as indeed are research participants, respondents, colleagues and friends. Thus people's behaviour is driven by political strategy, and this means that research in these settings can never be 'clean', 'neutral' or 'objective'. In order to create a meaningful piece of research researchers must acknowledge research itself as a political act; in itself part of the power relations that make up the workplace. Unfortunately this may have the consequence that, when power relations change, either through a change of personnel or a change of heart, the research becomes vulnerable. One person talked about the difficulties of going from a supportive research environment to a non-supportive one, as a result of a change in management imperatives:

> The new principal had very different ideas, he didn't value research … he really didn't want it at the college I think. And that's when I was made redundant … there is a niggle … as to whether it was part of the issue that we were identified as people to go … difficult to tell.
>
> (Sarah, post-compulsory manager)

We have suggested elsewhere (Drake & Heath, 2008) that the culture of research within an organisation may be a key element in the success of the doctoral researcher, and so it follows that researchers who are lecturers in higher education might expect to have a more supportive institutional culture of research-based practice than their school-based peers. However, this generalised view omits several significant points, not least of which is the tension between research and teaching for faculty in departments of education in higher education. Thus, ironically, researchers from a teacher-training-intensive department of education may find they have a less personally facilitative or supportive research culture within their particular faculty than a colleague at the same institution working in another area, even if the institution's policy is one of supporting research across the board.

Often vulnerable, insiders should understand that institutional politics may shift as a result of their actions, or as unintended consequences of their actions (Coghlan & Holian, 2007). The culture of research within an organisation may be a key element of success. It is not difficult to envisage the different experiences researchers may experience if they find themselves, on the one hand, in a supportive and encouraging environment underpinned by a strong institutional culture of research-based practice, or, on the other, in one which has a less constructive attitude to research.

For those lecturer-practitioners working in universities there may be particular sets of circumstances to confront. Doctoral researchers may have their research supervised by colleagues whilst simultaneously sustaining other relationships. Whilst undertaking my (Pat's) doctorate I was at the same time head of department in my university. This made me in effect the line manager of my doctoral supervisor and of my internal examiner, and the complicated relations of status and power needed careful navigation by all concerned, right up to the point of the doctoral viva where an additional external examiner was brought in to see fair play. This meant in effect defending independence, i.e. cultural dominance, of the doctoral degree awarding process, by ensuring that I would not be awarded the degree as a result of my status. Effectively this placed the doctoral degree at a higher institutional level than my professional practice, and this is consistent with the discussion in Chapter 2 about the privileging of academic knowledge.

Other university staff undertaking their studies alongside junior colleagues said that their colleagues had great difficulty in viewing them as anything other than their 'line manager'. Even on study days and in researcher action learning sets, conflict between being a practitioner and being a researcher was problematic for some:

> people would say, 'oh I'm glad I've seen you, I must catch you and ask you about X' ... the group used to have lunch together but I knew I would spend my time being asked questions about work so I used to take sandwiches and go and hide in the end.
>
> (Louisa, a university lecturer)

Inhabiting the hyphens

Hyphens populate the world of insider research! A colleague, Peter, himself undertaking a professional doctorate, encapsulated this by suggesting that what he is doing is 'inhabiting the hyphen'. There are several hyphens: insider-outsider, lecturer-practitioner, practitioner-researcher. Inhabiting the hyphens or some other hinterland as part of the researcher-practitioner continuum is one thing from the research perspective. From the professional perspective the occupant of these spaces is continuously aware of the potential of the research to raise professional problems that must also be addressed.

> There's issues of trust that have to be negotiated as well ... when you're actually getting deeper into processes with people ... that's fine for writing up an abstract assignment, but in your real job you then have to think 'what am I going to do about this?'
>
> (Jane, a university administrator, quoted in Drake & Heath, 2008: 135)

Of course, the relationship between research and professional life is not static. A doctoral degree takes five or six years to complete part-time, and it would be highly unusual for a person to remain in the same professional or personal position during that time. As well as unpredictable alterations in family or external factors, it is quite usual for jobs or personnel to change, and indeed some researchers deliberately court these changes in order to deal with problematic aspects of conducting their research, particularly writing it up. Some professional doctoral researchers begin by investigating practice outside their own workplace, and whilst this may ameliorate some of the tensions, it may raise other difficulties. One of these is access to the research setting, which may be particularly challenging for lecturer-practitioners entering the university from practice as teachers or social or health workers, as these researchers, in moving into university, have become professionally distanced from the setting in which they are very knowledgeable.

Insider researchers may change position, sometimes frequently, along axes with respect to both research and their professional practice. Hellawell (2006) argues that there are subtle and varying shades of 'insiderism' and it can sometimes become apparent that the same researcher slides along more than one insider-outsider continuum and in both directions, during the research process. Mercer (2007) asks whether being an insider refers to any or all of working in a shared place, having shared beliefs or speaking a common language with other professionals in the field. This work highlights the feelings of the researcher, and suggests that whilst an inexperienced researcher may be extremely conscious of position, this is not necessarily communicated to colleagues or other informants participating in the study. Gewirtz and Ozga (1994), experienced researchers reflecting on two sets of interviews they conducted with, respectively, senior ex-civil servants and single mothers, reinforce this. They were convinced that access to the senior ex-civil servants was only granted because they were perceived as harmless and because they were women, and this set up some discomfiture as the theoretical framework of the study (into decision-making by policy elites) was of radical feminism. However, these interviews were entirely comfortable social occasions, unlike the interviews with the single mothers where the conversations felt stilted and socially disjointed. Other contemporary commentators (for instance, Labaree, 2002) argue that it is possible to be to some extent simultaneously an insider and an outsider. For example, a woman interviewing women colleagues may share the common element of gender and collegiality but lack common experience on an age dimension, and, as in the example above, social class may determine the ease of the encounter. One of Hellawell's researchers focused on her understanding of these differing perspectives at various stages of her research, and this made her writing truly reflexive. She discusses research distances involved as her own employment position changed and her understanding of, and empathy with, her interviewees regarding their situation deepened.

Humphrey (2007) draws attention to the insider-outsider hyphen, suggesting that researchers can lose their sense of self if they are pulled one way or the other by being seen alternately as an insider or an outsider (depending on whether they are colleague, compatriot, friend or researcher). Humphrey writes of 'sliding along' or 'being shunted along' the insider-outsider continuum and 'suffering dissonances between self-identifications and other-attributions' (2007: 19). Humphrey contends that the acknowledgement of the insider-outsider hyphen is essential to researcher reflexivity. The insider-outsider researcher can be pushed and pulled along an invisible insider-outsider continuum by others who have a vested interest in who they are and what they are doing. Cast as 'insider' and as 'outsider' by different actors and audiences, she can 'lose sight of herself' (2007: 23). To actively take charge of the hyphen is to appreciate one's uniqueness as an insider-outsider and to cross over between communities. When researchers acknowledge moving on this continuum they are better placed to protect themselves and their projects from others (both insiders and outsiders). This is about taking charge, taking responsibility and defining the researcher's identity and defending their integrity. Thus the insider-outsider gives birth to a new world 'which occupies the space between the world of insider and of outsider' (2007: 23). This new identity emerges through wrestling with contradictions and tensions inherent in being both inside and outside. It is perhaps through reflective and reflexive writing that these issues can be best explored, examined and problematised.

Moore writes of seriously underestimating the impact his research would have at work, given that acquiring new insights and new understandings upset his own equilibrium and that of his colleagues. This led to him to question his contentment with his own privileged position. Moreover, when he came to write up his own doctorate he questioned the idea that writing reflectively and reflexively is relatively straightforward and instead described his thoughts and feelings as 'a cascade of mixed emotions ... that sufficiently well express the mix and multipleness of the perspectives and positions or the complexity of being an insider researcher' (2007: 35).

The implication is that insider researchers may anticipate future challenges to their professional position as directly or indirectly arising from having conducted insider research within their organisation.

Relationships with colleagues

Easy access to data through one's workplace is in tension with living with the providers of that data, and their thoughts and feelings about it. Working with colleagues whilst undertaking research means that practitioner doctorate researchers have to adopt complex positions in relation to people connected to their project whilst working with these people, perhaps even being in the same professional team. If data relates to particular individuals at work this can cause complications, both in terms of what the researcher then 'knows' about the colleague's work, and in terms of what the colleague thinks they know about the research or researcher; and what it is possible, or indeed ethical, to take further. Several participants in our study remark on the challenges of dealing with data that relates to colleagues. This is most obviously sensitive when it refers to the competence of colleagues, as one person said:

> I have had students who've said 'the other tutor taught me and it wasn't very good' ... I have a professional relationship with my colleague I need to maintain ... for a start I could never publish because he would be easily identifiable.
>
> (Alan, a university lecturer)

Another researcher acknowledged that senior players in his organisation would reveal one face to colleagues and subordinates in public, in meetings for example, and quite another in private when being interviewed 'confidentially' by the researcher. This raises another issue relating to the relationship of the practitioner researcher and the practice setting – how can researchers 'un-hear' things such as this? Of course they cannot. Insiders may feel beholden to those people had given up their time to participate in the research, and be unwilling to challenge or criticise their views. And friends and colleagues frequently want to help their novice researcher-colleague: a situation which one of the informants called 'saying nice things to help my research'. Researchers also told us about the 'suspicion' of some colleagues – not only of those within the same organisation. This came as rather a surprise, certainly to the individuals, who were not expecting research itself to be located quite so obviously as a management surveillance strategy. Quite reasonably colleagues of researchers in the same institution wanted to know the purpose of the research and who would see it; less expected were queries about the impact on informants' professional position of agreeing to participate. People researching practice in other organisations were sometimes treated as if they were undertaking research as a subterfuge for gaining insight about competitor's activities, as one confided: 'There were contacts who were very suspicious about what I was doing ... I felt that they felt I was some sort of spy, trying to get some inside information to use for our own benefit' (David, a university lecturer). People deal with who to involve in their research in different ways. For example, one head of department in a secondary school, conscious of the potential for exploitation, talked of making a decision not to talk to any junior members of staff for whose professional development he held responsibility, and neither would he talk to anyone in his own department since he believed they may feel that any controversial comments could impact negatively on professional performance management reviews. However, he regretted some of these decisions since in only talking to senior members of the institution he described his interviews as being 'only with people who are used to being in a position where they think care-fully about what they say'. The original intention had been to gauge the depth of feeling of a particular issue across the institution but because of his understanding of the restrictions on such insider research, he felt that his results were unreliable. Because power operates in different ways in organisations, for example pervading class and through gender relations, as well as through top-down management edicts, weaving an account of these relations through the 'findings' might provide a higher degree of authenticity than simply reporting them alone would do.

For lecturer-practitioners and other staff in higher education, there are additional complications, beginning with the potential for embar-rassment arising from doctoral work being assessed by one's colleagues. We were told by Louisa:

> And the other thing that got to me was that I felt they were all looking at my essay … because I know that's how we moderate … we get a bag of doughnuts and all the essays and a big cup of coffee … and I could see this room of people saying things like 'oh God, you wouldn't expect her to write like that'.

Assigning supervisors is also tricky for people within the same organisa-tion, for, whether real or imagined, insecurities are not hard to envisage if people who have, or who have had in the past, difficult professional relationships are then matched in the research. We have also recently had reported to us that the line manager of one of our practitioner doc-toral researchers, himself undertaking masters study on a similar topic at a different university, asked the doctoral researcher for her literature review to copy for his own masters dissertation. Technically this is not plagiarism, for unless the material is in the public domain, i.e. published, the intellectual property and copyright law does not apply. However, it is another indication of how institutional politics and power relations play out in behaviour in universities in relation to surveillance strategies for which 'research' provides fuel.

Becoming practitioner researcher

There are clear sets of difficulties in conducting a research study in one's own workplace in terms of the researcher's status within the institution and considerations regarding what the researcher represents to the other participants. Drake (2009) suggests that with this style of working comes privileged access to participants, although this comes with a health warning since the researcher must live with the consequences of their project, and ethical dimensions need careful consideration (see Chapter 5). Research in the workplace is likely to be small-scale and involve few people, so preserving confidentiality within the group is challenging and needs continual re-negotiation. Closeness to practice may compromise the researcher's ability to critically engage with the information and so a means of stimulating reflexivity such as keeping and using research diaries provides an important means of 'self-triangulation' of interpretations of the data. This is particularly important given that practitioners often choose their project as a result of being engaged with the issues they subsequently want to research for a number of years, and may well have a theoretical stance before beginning their research based on their assumptions and ideas about what they expect to find out. Eraut (1994) warns of difficulties in aligning situational, tacit, process and conceptual knowledge in a professional setting with a desire for neutrality as a researcher in the same setting. We too acknowledge the improbability of achieving a 'clean' research methodology, not least because in small-scale research within a single organisation, people talk to others that they know quite well and may be friendly with. Platt (1981) discusses in a seminal paper some of the challenges she faced when researching in her own workplace. Her main concern was precisely the difficulty in establishing a neutral persona. Drake (2010) places this difficulty in the context of the politics of the workplace, and argues that not only is it actually impossible to achieve neutrality, but also that there are gains from not doing so that compensate for this.

Table 3.1 presents this balance. We might read the left-hand column as showing the advantages that insiders bring to their project, and the right-hand column representing some of the challenges of this way of working. However, categorising too rigidly prevents the fluidity of position that, we are arguing, distinguishes insider research methodology, so it should be read with caution.

Table 3.1 shows clearly the compromises that the practitioner researcher must consider. On the one hand, knowledge of the setting and the people in it at first provide understanding, insider knowledge of power relations, access to people and to information and the opportunity to use one's own professional status to manage the research on one's own terms. However, this must be balanced by the politics of undertaking the research at all, the partisan and partial nature of choices and decisions that can impact not only on collegial relations in the workplace but also on the very nature of the work.

Hockey (1994) stresses the strengths of the insider researcher. For example, the advantages of researching in familiar settings may mean a relative lack of culture shock or disorientation and the possibility of enhanced rapport and communication, and an ability to gauge the honesty and accuracy of colleagues' responses. Hammersley (1993) asserts that no position guarantees valid knowledge, and no position prevents it either. There are no overwhelming advantages to being an

Table 3.1 SWOT analysis of benefits of insider research

Strengths	Weaknesses
Knowledge of organisation	Lose broader perspective
Established relationships	Lose element of neutrality/political
Collegial connections	Theoretical framework can be
Resources	influenced by dominant discourse
Immediacy/potential for impact on	or ideology
practice/immediate feedback	
Cost-effective	
Manageability	
Power	
Autonomy	
Opportunities	Challenges
Getting access to information	Internal resistance to process of
Getting access to people and	research
institutions	Reliability and validity
Manageability	Identity as a researcher
	Work–research balance, loyalties and
	values
	Relationships with colleagues could
	become contentious
	Power

insider or an outsider and each position has advantages and disadvantages, though these will vary depending on the particular circumstances and purposes of the research. Practitioner doctoral researchers recognise that their access to a research setting is privileged, enabling them to contact colleagues either within their own organisation or outside it that they might not otherwise have been able to reach. 'That gave me licence to go and see other schools. You think you can just ring up and pop over and go, but you can't, but if you've got research in a way that gives you access' (George, a primary school headteacher).

In recognising that professional doctoral students develop multiple identities with respect to work, research and practice, we must also recognise that they also develop what might be termed 'multiple integrities'. Professional doctorate degrees target 'senior professionals' (Heath, 2005), and such individuals have loyalties to their workplace, regardless of what the research uncovers, as well as deepening awareness of what research integrity must entail, especially in the case of small-scale projects. This quest for research integrity necessitates an exploration of validity as a concept, and in a project in one's own workplace this exploration involves recognising both that the research is not replicable and the need to place oneself as an active participant in the study. We found, although numbers are far too small to generalise, various means of dealing with this problem, including in-depth consideration of research as narrative enquiry (Drake, 2006); changing jobs after undertaking fieldwork; or, having realised the challenges of having one's colleagues as research participants, deciding to conduct the major project outside their immediate workplace. The higher a practitioner researcher is placed in their employing organisation, the better positioned they may be to place research significantly on their agenda, and find time to do it, without compromising their practice. However, in our study, people who had completed their doctorates recognise that managing time successfully does not just happen by chance. Writing is done at the weekends and in school holidays and to strict, self-imposed deadlines. Managing time to study whilst holding down a full-time managerial position, maintaining close family and extended family relationships, dealing with unexpected interruptions to study such as a change in job responsibilities (Bourner *et al.*, 2001; Blaxter *et al.*, 2001) or, more problematically and less predictably, managing health problems all present significant difficulties.

Being a practitioner doctoral researcher undertaking research as an insider may feel like a paradoxical experience. The researcher may feel inclined to try to separate professional identity from research identity. Such dilemmas sometimes lead to researchers changing the direction of their research in order to accommodate these twin positions separately. Yet we contend that it is through a merging of these functions that the person develops their unique and applicable perspective on their research project. The need for this integration is apparent from the very early stages of practitioner research, and has implications for methodology and ethical choices as well as for the ways that the practitioner researcher learns what it means to undertake research at doctoral level. These are discussed in the following chapters in this book.

Chapter 4

Approaching grounded methodology

Professionals undertaking doctoral research have loyalties to their workplace, as well as deepening awareness of the need to develop research integrity and critical distance. This can lead to tension, for reconciling their position as both a researcher and as a responsible practitioner pitches researchers into a place that forces methodological as well as ethical consideration of researcher distance. We address ethical issues in Chapter 5. In this chapter we discuss fluidity in research-practitioner positioning, and what this means in terms of research integrity, validity and objectivity. For insider research is conducted alongside professional relationships, sometimes on the back of these; and what the research uncovers has to be lived with in the professional setting. In our study we found various means of dealing with this tension. For instance, some people may change jobs deliberately between their field work and writing it up so as to leave behind the site of the inquiry and cloak the tension by anonymising it. Others, realising the challenges of having one's colleagues as research participants, decide to conduct major enquiries outside the immediate workplace. Unfortunately neither of these tactics avoids the central challenges arising out of the researcher being deeply involved in the professional practices that are the site of the inquiry.

The positions that insider researchers establish in order to deal with the problems of being inextricably linked with the methods they use in practices that they are engaged in are fluid and not methodologically static. Researcher position is, at any time during the conduct of the project, relative to what is happening in the project. We seek to justify this through recourse to scrutiny of scientific inductive approaches over time, and point to discontinuities regarding shared understanding of scientific method. We suggest that as it is the researcher's voice that explains the research, based as this is on the expressed views of the participants with whom they may be in complex relations, grounded theory paves the way for a further step into what might be called grounded methodology.

Methodological attitude to inquiry

'Scientific method' itself has shifted over millennia from non-interventionist observations of the early astronomers and navigators to the direct and targeted attempts to create, make or explain that characterised science and technological development in the 200 years or so leading up to the twentieth century. This direct intervention attempted, arguably with considerable success, to control variables, to predict, to isolate and to develop a concept of probabilistic association that enabled statistical verification of observable phenomena and events. It is difficult to evade the obvious realities of inventions such as electricity or polymer plastic, of transport systems that include space travel. And it is humbling to recognise that without apparatus or easy means of communication early science was able correctly to deduce the solar and planetary systems. Science currently is enthralled by quantum theory and string theory, and this shift to a theoretical perspective on the universe has to some extent separated science from technology.

Thomas Kuhn (1970) famously questioned the objectivity of scientific method, placing the science that is selected for investigation (as opposed to the potential science that is not), the way that it is conducted and what happens to train scientists to conduct research, into a framework that is totally contingent on the prevailing scientific culture, or paradigm, of the moment. Periodically, argues Kuhn, there is a 'scientific revolution', triggered by discontinuities or occurrences or phenomena which cannot be explained satisfactorily by prevailing theory. Far from science developing in a linear, objective way, with knowledge being developed in the paradigm of previous knowledge, Kuhn describes a tempestuous culture where changes of paradigm have momentous impact on the way science is conducted. Positivism, i.e. empirical activity that seeks not to negate hypotheses regarding potential scientific 'truths', can be viewed in Kuhnian terms as a scientific paradigm which may be possibly be overturned in a further 'revolution'.

Difficulties in maintaining particle metaphors for scientific concepts such as atoms and molecules have led science in the recent past to develop new perspectives. These perspectives recognise overall uncertainty – indeed Heisenberg's (1927) uncertainty principle states that it is impossible to correctly measure the velocity and mass of an electron at the same time because the one will affect the other (see, for example, Cassidy, 1992). And scientists now talk freely about 'parallel universes' that exist and behave differently and quite unpredictably in relation to each other.

The way was paved in the late twentieth century for a serious challenge to the concepts of logical positivist research. In their seminal book *Naturalistic Inquiry*, Lincoln and Guba (1985) stake out the territory in the social sciences, where it was recognised that variables are much more difficult to control. Nearly half of the book's 416 pages are devoted to a deconstruction and critique of logical positivism as applied to scientific research. Loaded chapter titles – for example, 'The only generalisation is: there is no generalisation' – and a collection of weird scenarios imagined by scientists are assembled to provide counter-examples to established positivist concepts, for example, 'Schrödinger's cat'. Schrödinger posited an unlikely singleton atom that has a 50–50 chance of self-destruction in a sealed container. If the atom destructs, a poisonous gas is released. The question is, if a cat is placed in the container also, would it, after an hour, be alive or dead? The point, readers are informed, is that whether the cat is alive or dead is unknown, but that in our minds we can entertain both outcomes equally and imagine feelings and consequences for each. Thus, argues Schrödinger and like-minded scientists, we must take multiple perspectives on the universe; there is not a single correct point of view.[1] There are, of course, more meaningful reasons for adopting multiple perspectives! The challenge that Lincoln and Guba embrace is to critique logical positivism using scientific examples, thus establishing a more general case for 'naturalistic inquiry'. Thomas Kuhn may himself have termed the emergence of their book as part of a 'scientific revolution' in itself.

However, Chalmers warns of an 'anything goes' approach to science:

> For if this view is adopted it is liable to lead to a situation in which those who already have power keep it. As John Krige has put it, in a way that I wish I had thought of myself, 'anything goes' means in practice that 'everything stays'.

(1982: 144)

What does validity mean in practitioner research?

As discussed in Chapter 3, people at work in public service institutions operate in intensely political climates. The prevailing ideologies may allow for little dissent, and create hegemonies for practice that can be analysed in terms of the distribution of power through networks and maintaining dominance. In researching one's own workplace one is necessarily positioned by these prevailing political ideologies, as are one's research respondents, colleagues, friends, etc. Thus people's behaviour is driven by political stratagem, and so the research can never be 'clean', 'neutral', 'objective'. Attempts to cope with this difficulty have been described in various ways, for example, Whitehead and McNiff (2006) discuss the possibility of practitioner researchers at doctoral level creating 'living theories' that arise out of their explicit and particular circumstances and which, unlike the propositional knowledge that usually dominates, challenge the status quo of knowledge itself. Living theories or 'grounded methodologies' question what it means to know. Researchers at doctoral level questioning this knowledge base are also challenging institutional power bases, and this means taking a risk that may bring repercussions onto the researcher. Thus practitioner researchers are in need of methodological tools to help construct a justifiable and authentic defence of a partial and knowing research position, and this means taking a reflexive stance. In other words, placing oneself squarely in the frame of the research and considering explicitly what that means for the project provides a degree of integrity and authenticity.

The extent to which researchers put themselves squarely in the frame of the research has been of significant interest for some time, particularly for qualitative researchers, and is frequently discussed in the context of the deconstruction movements. Postmodernist educational writers (e.g. Schostak, 2000; MacLure, 2003) develop the idea of reflexivity and this leads to a theoretical position whereby any text purporting to describe, report on or analyse events in the world inevitably does so only as an interpretation in recognition that the text stands as a mediator between the author (who is indescribable) and the 'Other', i.e. outside the author, also indescribable.

With the trends for professional doctorate degrees come fresh practical concerns facing insider researchers, particularly when researching one's own practice, as is likely in the early stages of practitioner research. There are potentially clear sets of difficulties to recognise in conducting a research study in one's workplace in terms of status and what the researcher represents to the practices and people engaging in them. Yet with this style of working comes very privileged access to the informants or participants, although the researcher at work must live with the consequences of their project (Mercer, 2007).

Insider researchers are often attracted by three specific methodologies: grounded theory, action research and case study. Grounded theory, whereby a theoretical position emerges through interrogation of the data, is usually attributed to Glaser and Strauss (1987). Action research, whereby an iterative cycle of change or adaptation to the context arises from the investigation, arose out of an approach to evaluation studies known as 'responsive' evaluations (see, for example, Carr & Kemmis, 1986; Stake, 1981) that emerged as part of positivist critique in applied educational research. Ethnographic researchers immerse themselves in the detail of a few respondents and produce 'thick descriptions' (Geertz, 1973; Hammersley & Atkinson, 1995), both descriptive and interpretive, so as to ascribe some significance to the observations without gathering broad, statistical information. Insiders developing data sets from in-depth participation, possibly also including some intervention and/or development, are persuaded that their approach, drawn upon ethnographic traditions, may fit within an action research paradigm and can be presented as case study, and indeed up to a point it can.

Practitioner researchers may be searching for methodologies that enable them to be simultaneously practitioner and researcher, unlike the methodological discourses that sustain a distinction between the 'investigator' and the 'respondents', the 'researcher' and 'practice', respondents and reality, 'because it is their constructions of reality that the inquirer seeks to reconstruct' (Lincoln & Guba, 1985: 41). These issues immediately take the insider researcher study into a realm of abstraction requiring deep and detailed consideration, for it may be impossible to sustain distinctions between 'researcher' and 'researched' when one is so deeply involved in the practices that are being investigated. Losing these anchors takes the participants in the study into slippery territory. For without the anchors, what might the research achieve? What claims is the researcher empowered to make? These questions are in themselves research questions, part of each and every insider research project, and become a quest for research integrity. Necessarily this means exploring validity as a concept that applies in the case of the project; and in a project in one's own workplace, this exploration involves recognising both that the research is not replicable and the need to place oneself as an active participant in the study.

Research validity is a concept deriving from statistical investigation and refers to research finding out about what it aims to find out about. 'Internal validity' is jeopardised when undertaking the investigation itself affects in immeasurable ways the behaviour of the subjects of the investigation. External validity is concerned with the extent to which the results of statistical research can be generalised to a wider population. Both forms of validity can be maximised in various ways by taking account of the various factors known to be threats, for example, researcher and research effect of testing, or interviewing, or choice of sample, or loss of concentration on the part of the researcher. However, underpinning the concept of statistical validity is the idea that there is a 'truth' that the research is aiming to uncover, however slippery that truth is to get at.

Lather is a feminist research methodologian concerned about the validity of research. She comments on 'the failure of positivism', because of what she calls a reality crisis in physics: 'We live in both/and worlds full of paradox and uncertainty, where close inspection turns unities into multiplicities, clarities into ambiguities, univocal simplicities into polyvocal complexities' (1991: xvi). Thus, as the very essence of science, physics, now seems multi-dimensional and uncertain, conventional scientific method, positivist inquiry, is no longer the only appropriate means for investigating it. Objectivity is unattainable even in this domain which it has served for so long. Eraut (2003) also disengages science from positivist objectivity, according scientific status simply to work that appears in print. Whilst located in the postmodern, Lather is sympathetic to science and scientific knowledge, which, by presenting clearly the problems of scientific research, she is able to show is also consistent with a postmodern paradigm. Thus she is able to encompass concepts of rigour and validity, and suggest what they may look like in the light of 'anti-foundational discourse theory'. As explained earlier, post-modernism points to an absence of established knowledge, showing us that context, content and voice are all relative to each other and position 'reality' relationally. Like or hate postmodernism, it does create a dis-course which enables us to scrutinise research activities. Lather re-formulates and positions validity as 'a space of constructed visibility of the practices of methodology' (1993: 674) which enables research to scrutinise its own methods of making meaning. She explains that if there are no agreed foundations or truths then the 'principles of legitimation' (or why we might give the work some credibility) need to be explicitly 'articulated, ratified and put into practice'.

In other words, an attempt to identify essential knowledge out of research is a misplaced quest. Notwithstanding this, Lather argues that research as a means of critical reflection is a worthwhile process. Her 'Notes towards self-critique' are a step towards uncovering what the research does and does not privilege.

1   Did I encourage ambivalence and multiplicity, or did I impose order and structure?
2   What is most densely invested? What has been muted, repressed, unheard? Have I confronted my own evasions?
3   Did I create a text that was multiple without being pluralistic, double without being paralysed?
4   Did I focus on the limits of my own conceptions?
5   Who are my Others? What binaries structure my argument? What hierarchies are at play? Have I imagined a space that would contain only subjects: no more spectators, only actors, all similarly compro-mised, with no possible exceptions?
6   Did I make resistant discourses and subject positions widely available?
7   How was this work tied into the demands of my academic career?

(Adapted from 1991: 84)

The overall challenge seems to be to come to terms with how to devise practitioner research that investigates experience, understands and describes it in such a way so as to be recognisably worthwhile, whilst appreciating simultaneously that this may be theoretically impossible. This search is for theoretical integrity and purpose, i.e. an approach that enables the practitioner researcher to understand and cope with a position that is integrated with a professional persona. There are research limitations to accept in being in this position, whilst simultaneously proposing that in terms of professional study, this is an honest position to take, that research is genuine, authentic, is researching what it purports to be researching. Professionals have very privileged access to research subjects which may provide some virtue to the research process – however, it may not be possible to gain any sense of distance, and conventional methods of checking and triangulation seem elusive without abusing the time or patience of the research subjects.

Distinctions between academic, applied and activist research have been explored by Leonard (2001). Table 4.1 shows how this works. These distinctions are helpful in pointing to possible tensions for researchers when formulating what the research is for: is it to expand the boundaries of knowledge, or is it to solve a practical problem, or perhaps the research is conceived as emancipatory, that is, aiming to change the world through heightened understanding? As the table clearly shows, the purpose of the research affects everything about it: the way it is positioned in the context and conducted; the approach taken and the stance of the researcher; and the means by which the research knowledge comes to view. This is an important way of considering research activity, for a direct implication of this perspective is that finding 'the truth' becomes secondary to the extent to which the research is fit for purpose.

Social science writers about educational research (e.g. Ball, 1990; Schostak, 2000; MacLure, 2003) seem preoccupied with a binary polarity between qualitative and positivist/scientific research. Qualitative research attempts a more closely grained look at what 'really happened' (e.g. Goodson, 1992). Positivist or scientific research, on the other hand, moves away from detail towards 'verifiable' findings, where verifiable means that the research has been conducted cleanly, objectively and in such a manner as to be replicable by another researcher under similar conditions. As is pointed out frequently, this degree of objectivity is unrealistic. The purpose of the research and who is sponsoring it are significant in establishing methodological position regarding developing new knowledge through the project. So, for instance, research that is commissioned by government for policy purposes is highly probably positioned differently from action research aiming to change practice for the better within an educational setting, yet both might adopt qualitative and quantitative methods.

Some people would explain that 'scientific' currently means 'published', and this discourse is evident through, for example, databases such as 'Web of Science' that includes social science. This discourse effectively disengages science from positivist objectivity which in any

Table 4.1 Types of research

	Academic research	Applied or policy research	Activist research
Problem formulation	Original Making an important contribution to knowledge	Commissioned Solving a practical problem or with a practical application	Empowering Understanding the world in order to change it (so as to help the less powerful)
Context	Universal What could be changed	Local What can be changed	Politically engaged What should be changed
Role	Detached Public intellectual	Hierarchical Values and responsibilities from top down	Participatory Democratic decisions with participants
Methodology	Rational, sceptical Concerned with epistemology and methodologically correct practices	Expert Hired to provide information, on time and under budget	Standpoint Ideas come from political struggle Empathetic and ethical concern for subjects
Presentation	Communal Stress on freedom to publish worldwide	Proprietary Knowledge owned by funder Evaluated by effectiveness	Accessible Accountable to a specific constituency

Source: Leonard (2001: 155).

case, according to Giddens (1977), has become a term of abuse. Seen from a Kuhnian perspective, scientific in this sense can be interpreted as reflecting the times or culture or prevailing paradigms of research methods. However, other views prevail as well, so the matter cannot be completely dodged. For example, education policy research training would include statistical training in order to serve the needs of policy researchers. A doctoral thesis in this territory would involve counting or measuring the implementation or impact of policy, in other words taking an objectively empirical approach to data collection.

Researchers must deal with the struggle to continue their research in a professional setting in which they must also be aligned with the institutional aim of sustained or bettered reputation and increased funding. Thus, research as a whole tends to be located towards the central column of Table 4.1 of being externally funded and commissioned. However, individual academics fight to sustain knowledge and the right to pursue knowledge for its own sake (as characterised in the left-hand column), or as a means of promoting change (right-hand column). The doctoral programme is one site for this struggle, as expectation of an 'original contribution to knowledge' is a criterion for a successful thesis. To pursue a polarity between qualitative and quantitative research is to miss this point, as both are located within the same paradigm of research policy, which currently in the public services is government-driven. Both grapple with the same problems, the main one for each being a problem of veracity and fitness of voice with respect to the purpose of the research.

It seems that this forms the crux of a serious problem in educational research, particularly in professional settings or related to professional contexts. That is, for education research to be commissioned it must be useful or applied and have implications for policy, as such needs must be technical and draw inferences from observed phenomena, and in this traditional sense be scientific. On the other hand, inherent difficulties in collecting and interpreting data in this way are recognised potentially to compromise the integrity of the research process and the researchers who conduct it, should they stick to a paradigm that prioritises objective, often numerical data. How individuals cope with this dilemma is significant in positioning them within the academy. Funding from research bodies that are sympathetic to scrutiny of process as well as policy is extremely difficult to acquire. Thus, anyone intending to pursue educational research from within a university and to build a creditable reputation for doing so must place themselves in such a position as to be able to skip adroitly between the descriptors set out in the three columns in Table 4.1.

Lincoln and Guba make some bold claims for naturalistic inquiries, which include the following:

1 They are in natural settings, as the wholes cannot be understood in isolation from their contexts.
2 Humans gather primary data because only humans are capable of grasping and evaluating meaning during data gathering.
3 Naturalistic inquiries utilise tacit knowledge, because there are tacit interactions between investigators and respondents, and because tacit knowledge mirrors the value patterns of the investigator.
4 They prefer qualitative methods because these are more adaptable to the multiple realities pertaining to the circumstances.
5 They sample purposively in order to gather as much data as is possible.
6 They analyse data through induction, because this makes interactions explicit, describes settings fully, makes transferability to other settings easier, identifies mutually shaping influences. Values can be an explicit part of the analytic process.
7 Theory is grounded in data because no a priori theory could encompass multiple generalisations, and because shapings in a context may be completely explicable in terms of the context.
8 Research design emerges through the study rather than being predictable in advance.
9 Meanings are negotiated with the respondents 'because it is their constructions of reality that the inquirer seeks to reconstruct'.
10 Reports are case studies.
11 Representations are ideographic, in other words, arising from the contexts and not from underlying laws or rules. Thus, application of the research must be tentative and not overly generalised as this would be inappropriate.
12 There are special criteria for trustworthiness of the work: is it credible, transferable, dependable and can it be confirmed?

(Adapted from Lincoln & Guba, 1985: 39–43)

Case study is an approach to research frequently adopted when researchers are faced with a specific instance. Case study as a means of gathering and writing about data came to prominence in the mid-1970s when a group of researchers engaged in evaluation highlighted the approach as providing data that is 'strong in reality' (see, for example, Adelman *et al.*, 1976; Simons, 1980; Burgess, 1984, 1985). Case studies, although critiqued for providing an account of a unique circumstance that it is not possible to replicate, have the very great strength that they are based on empirical data that is gathered through observation. Different types of observation are possible, with observers taking a 'participant' or 'non-participant' position and dealing with the attendant challenges arising from that position. So, participant observers make a choice whether or not to reveal their identity and purpose to those being observed, according to their view as to how the 'reality' being studied would change with explicit knowledge of the research. Several studies in the 1970s and early 1980s were conducted (see, for example, Burgess, 1984) whereby the researcher kept their purpose covert, and this approach stimulated subsequent 'confessional tales' (see, for example, Ball, 1990) once the researchers had grown up and reflected on the possibility that this hide-and-seek approach in educational settings was at best disrespectful to the participants and, at worst, unethical. Non-participant observation poses different challenges, as the researcher in a setting has to find a means of conducting the observations without also disturbing the setting, and without interfering in the activities forming the primary purpose. So, for example, my (Pat's) colleague, when observing in classrooms, played a part of 'less adult' (Pryor, 2000) so as to convey to the children and the teachers that he is not there to teach and that he is not part of the behaviour-management strategy. Case studies may not aim to be generalisable beyond the context of the study, but they surely aim to (re)present as nearly as possible a 'reality' of the research context.

The insider researcher is seeking to express, not the respondents' version of reality, but their own, even though this will often be based on the expressed perspectives of respondents who may also be colleagues and friends. Thus the insider researcher may be seeking a methodological position that enables them to integrate researcher and practitioner functions, for these to merge into a new state of personal identity and action.

Putting oneself in the frame

Putting oneself squarely in the frame of the research has over the last couple of decades or so become an ethical consideration for qualitative researchers. Researchers writing at doctoral level face a choice in a sense that other researchers do not. Frequently, research as discussed earlier in this chapter is commissioned for a purpose that precludes much of a reflexive stance regarding the process of undertaking the work, and it is later on that researchers reveal their thoughts and feelings about the process. For example, Brackenridge (2001) conducted a 'neutral' study into understanding and preventing sexual exploitation in sport. In fact, conducting the study was very problematic as it raised issues regarding sexuality that it would have been inappropriate, she felt, to bring into the commissioned report, but that she later discusses. Doctoral researchers, however, are expected to include a full discussion of their methodology, and so at an early stage of the research are likely to make a decision as to whether to conduct the field work in their own workplace or elsewhere. There are very good reasons for choosing either route and in the thesis the author must defend the choices made in this regard.

Discussion about the place of the researcher in the research process is frequently located within a discursive, seemingly more qualitative framework of social science research (see, for example, Goodson, 1992; Miller, 1993). For a complete picture, logically we should also think about researcher position in the context of social or educational research into all disciplines, and indeed explorations of position with respect to research in the conventionally empiricist paradigms such as mathematics and science education have been undertaken by some feminist theorists (e.g. Harding, 1986; Dunne & Johnson, 1994). Harding undertakes a challenging critique of science in order to find a way of locating women within the gendered, empiricist approach that appears to neutralise scientific inquiry but which in fact assures the discourse as masculinist through the coercive values, such as racism, sexism, classism, that deteriorate objectivity. Dunne and Johnson take a critical look at research into gender dimensions of mathematics education. They describe projects as being technical, bringing out quantitative descriptions of sex differences, or explanatory studies which appeal to biology, or social explanations that lead to strategies about changing curriculum, or how not to sex stereotype. They argue that both these approaches assume neutrality of the researcher, and also put girls at disadvantage with respect to mathematics by taking an essentialist approach to the subject, for example, positioning girls as cooperative when mathematics is a competitive discourse.

Feminists have argued for emancipatory research which emancipates equally the researcher, researched and the discourse of the field of investigation. From the third column of Table 4.1, it is evident that research that is emancipatory is also driven by an agenda of change, of making things better. This is fraught with problems; for the development of research approaches which empower those involved to change as well as understand the world produces metaphors which produce binaries: to 'enlighten' (Derrida, 1982) positions emancipators as senders and emancipated as receivers of light. Clearly there are value judgements inherent in such desire to emancipate, with individuals at either end of the binary having potentially different priorities. And power, according to the theoretical analysis above, is inherent in structures that privilege some individuals, and is rarely given away 'to'; it is much more likely to be wrested away 'from' after an arduous struggle. Thus research that seeks to 'empower' participants should be regarded with caution, and with a critical eye on the extent of the power transformations.

The reason that this is so important again relates to the authenticity of both the project and any writing that emerges from it for there is a tension to be addressed. Participants in a research setting based in professional practice all have a stake in that practice which is not unknown for any of them. Thus, bringing participants into the creation of a research agenda seems on the face of it to be desirable so as to legitimate the inquiry. However, the stimulus for the doctoral project is likely to come from the researcher as it is she who must make the 'contribution to knowledge', with professional positioning conferring a further layer of complexity. Any agenda for change, development or 'liberation' is quite likely to be prompted by the dominant discourse of power, i.e. in the case of education research a hegemonic discourse emanating from education policy, combined with relations in the workplace as a result of gender, ethnicity, class, status, age, etc.

Becoming reflexive

Thus the search for method becomes a search for a means of critical reflexivity within the circumstances, and becomes an aspect of the project methodology. Criteria for trustworthiness – credibility, transferability, dependability and confirmability (Lincoln & Guba, 1985) – become critical and methodologically necessary, and in recognising the problems of position, it is important to take an explicit stance with respect to authorship of the text. This question of authorship and 'authority' of the textual account is critically linked to the methodological stance, for it is through text that critical reflexion is mediated. As we have shown, in the absence of positional benchmarks for the researcher to align with, reflexivity is a critical element of the methodology. So important is the relation of writing to the research process that it is discussed in detail in Chapter 9.

That the methodology is grounded and integrates data-gathering activity with constructing a text for it to live on in is a very relativist position to take, leading to a position of research in relation to practice, academically compromised by significant power relations, but compensated for by professional processes and insights arising out of the process of investigation and reflexion.

Gramsci (1971) has observed that every relationship of hegemony is an educative relationship, and therefore education is crucial in securing consent for the ruling way of life, especially prevailing mode of production. This immediately creates a tension, for researcher responsibilities to the 'prevailing mode of production' are to the knowledge-producing university, and these must co-exist with professional responsibilities to colleagues, participants and oneself to conduct research with integrity and to be awarded a doctoral degree.

It may be helpful to think about the problem of position in education research being analogous to the coastline and the tide. The researcher(s) need to decide (a) empirically how far away will give an approximation that is good enough for the purpose, and (b) theoretically how what is seen or experienced from the chosen distance can be explained or theorised sufficiently to help us recognise what we wouldn't otherwise know. To view or perhaps travel along the coastline we step further away and allow ourselves to approximate the details by using a scale to help us deal with the unimaginably long and unnecessarily detailed perturbations. The scale of our map depends upon our distance and speed, and it is this map that is the metaphor for empirical position. But to see or build the sandcastle or participate in the cricket and understand how the form of the shore affects our game we must be there at the time before the water washes the opportunity away. If we are not there, we have to rely on the simulacrum of a photograph or a memory, for of these occurrences there are no relics. It is this photograph that is equivalent to the theorised account, because just as in a photograph what is in the picture and whether it is recognised by the participants depends upon choices made by the photographer, so the credibility of the account is contingent on the voice of the author.

Chapter 5

Thinking about ethical considerations

In recent times, ethical considerations in research have become an integral element of each and every research proposal and study. Partly this is as a direct result of public sensibilities regarding the limits of inquiry, and partly as a result of legislation regarding human rights and data protection that originates from the same concerns. Doctoral researchers must address the conventions for ethical processes that prevail in the higher education institution in which they are registered as well as possibly needing to apply for ethical clearance from their employer to conduct their research. In this chapter we show that this is complicated, as professionals conducting research may be working within a framework of professional codes of conduct that are also subject to the law. In the intersections between professional and research ethical practices challenges and dilemmas arise for the insider researcher. At institutional levels, ethical practices and processes may be formalised and conventional, as indeed may be professional codes of conduct. The researcher, however, is in a position of developing an ethical perspective that is situated in and arises from the research in context. Importantly this is informed by the personal ethical values that researchers bring to their studies, as well as by the various ethical codes and practices that are in place.

This leads to considering ethics from perspective of situatedness. Rather than from a perspective that endorses the notion that ethical positions reflect objective or universal truths, instead these ethical considerations are related to the researcher's social, cultural, historical, personal and professional circumstances, which of course change over time and over the course of the study. Insider researchers are members of an organisation with a particular culture, ethos and workplace mission. They are most often also senior professionals who have loyalty to their workplace, regardless of what the work uncovers. They must handle interpersonal relationships very sensitively and may find that what comes after the doctoral project is of equal concern to what happens during the study, not least in terms of the security of their own jobs and their continuing personal and professional relationships with colleagues.

Background to ethical processes

Modern ethical approaches derived from the approach developed for use in the extremely sensitive Nuremberg Trials (1949) as a means of assessing whether experimentation on humans was or had been ethically justified. The Nuremberg Code asserted that participants in such research should give voluntary consent, be free from coercion and be able to withdraw at any time, having first understood through clear information the purpose of the research and the methods that would be used. The development of research ethics resulted in acceptance that anyone conducting research should follow the conventions of participants' confidentiality, anonymity and the right to withdraw.

The Nuremberg Code acted as an important staging post in the development of ethical practices. The medical ethics enshrined in the Hippocratic Oath, believed to have been written in the fifth century BCE and which medical practitioners still swear today, can be seen as the first principles of ethical practice in which nonmaleficence, or do no harm, is a starting point for appropriate professional behaviour. Research behaviour, however, had not been considered in this way until Nuremberg. In the field of medicine, various examples highlight the importance of proper ethical screening of research, from the development of the proposal to dissemination and implementation of the findings. For example, the drug thalidomide that, in a period of about four years, was prescribed to pregnant women to help cure morning sickness was later associated and finally correlated with thousands of birth defects worldwide. This case generated recognition that, before being licensed, drugs should be trialled carefully.

Another important project that led to explicit principles for research concerning and involving people was the controversial Tuskegee syphilis experiment in the US. In this study, African-American sharecroppers with syphilis were recruited and were tracked for a 40-year period from 1932 to 1972 to follow the natural development of the disease. Well intentioned, this research project aimed to discern whether sufferers were better off without the treatments for syphilis that, at the beginning of the study, were unpleasant, poisonous and dangerous, and brought uncertain benefit. However, penicillin became the standard treatment for syphilis during the course of the study and, despite the possibility of incorporating treatment by penicillin into it, the researchers continued the trial as originally conceived, with the result that many patients died and children were born with congenital syphilis. A leak to the press in 1972 led to the termination of the research. An immediate inquiry was set up and in 1979 the Belmont Report (Harms, 1979) was published. This report explicitly addressed the need for ethical principles in both biomedical and behavioural research, setting these out as three standards:

respect for persons; beneficence, i.e. greatest gain for the research with minimal risks to research subjects; and justice for participants and potential participants in so far as procedures should be thought through, equitable and not exploitative.

However, even insider or action research may trigger, sustain or reinforce a regime of oppression, intended or not, real or imagined. The Milgram (1974) 'obedience to authority' experiments arising out of Nuremberg show how classic laboratory-type research in the pursuit of knowledge and truth can be intrinsically very unethical, in this case duping naive subjects to apparently inflicting increasing pain on helpless victims; and the Stanford simulated role-play prison experiment in 1971 (where nominated prisoners from a group of volunteers rapidly become real abused victims of nominated warders, also volunteers) was for ethical reasons rapidly abandoned by the morally attuned and disgusted psychologist Philip Zimbardo because of the rapid onset of a regime of brutality.

The examples discussed illustrate three philosophical approaches in play when thinking about making moral or ethical decisions: virtue ethics, deontological ethics and consequentialist ethics. A 'virtue approach' (Aristotelian in origin) focuses on people's character rather than on compliance with a set of rules. Deontological ethics are concerned with moral duty, and consequentialist ethics with rational connections between the application of moral principle and the outcome. Specification of ethical practices is in this territory. It is in the absence of natural 'virtue' that contemporary moral codes for practice and for research have been developed. Deontic paradigms are identified with formal codified research protocols dictating what a researcher can and cannot do and hence must obey and follow irrespective of situation (e.g. always obeying the confidentiality clause even when it might be simply immoral). In consequentialist paradigms the researcher is concerned about instrumentally achieving pre-determined research outcomes and needs to work out the best course of action to achieve them. It is the goal of contemporary ethical thinking to produce virtuous practice, even though the manifestation of these intentions is deontic and consequentialist. As Webster states, this is 'a predictive formula which presupposes that cause and effect are eminently controllable' (2010).

So the 'moral duty' of research not to privilege the research over the experience of participants becomes the focus of criticism in the Tuskegee experiment; and the consequence of not observing a moral approach is inherent in the thalidomide tragedy.

Aristotle distinguishes further between sophia (wisdom) and phronesis. Sophia is the power to think about the way the world is, and has been equated therefore with science, although this may be a contestable distinction, for the science of Aristotle's time was inductive (Geertz, 2001) and based almost entirely on the power of the imagination, rather than deductive and using experimentation to test the imagination as today. Phronesis is variously translated as practical wisdom, common sense or prudence; it brings together knowledge with experience, and is concerned with issues of value and power.

In this chapter we show that ethical considerations in research may, for the insider researcher, engender tensions with professional practice that must be continually negotiated and re-negotiated, and lived with beyond the life of the study. Insider researchers at doctoral level usually study part-time whilst working full-time in the profession that then becomes the focus of their study. This means that in managing their location as 'insiders' they may necessarily change positions, sometimes frequently, along axes with respect to both their research and their professional practice. Action research – a preferred approach for much practitioner research at doctoral level – requires the researcher to negotiate being insider-outsider at the same time, and these researchers adopt a range of complex positions in relation to people connected to their study and move through them in a much more fluid way. We suggest that phronesis most aptly describes this, that in developing an ethical approach to insider research, the researcher needs to engage their own resources of knowledge and experience to help think through the conflicts, tensions and dilemmas that arise. Whilst there are no correct versions of how tensions should be resolved, there are reflexive pointers to thinking about them that can help the researcher determine what to do at the time.

Professional ethics

Professional ethics, first established in medicine, have become enshrined in other public service professions, such as social work and teaching. Often recast as 'Codes of practice' or 'Standards', these serve not only to protect the people who are on the receiving end of professional ministrations, but also as regulatory devices by which professional behaviour or misbehaviour can be judged. These codes usually focus mainly on the practices in which the professional engages with clients or users, less on the practices that professionals engage with between themselves. Accepting that adherence to a professional code is generally an explicit dimension of becoming a member of a professional group, and implementation of the code is understood usually to be the responsibility of the profession. For this purpose groups are set up as regulatory professional bodies, thus, for example, in the UK, the General Medical Council, the Law Society, the General Social Care Council, the General Teaching Council, and so on. This concept of self-regulation on the face of it seems consistent with the notion of the autonomous professional, someone whose actions spring from trained judgement, and someone who knows what to do.

In considering the professional ethics set out in these codes of practice we ought also to note their deontic nature – what practices, processes and expectations they are designed to achieve. For whilst codes of practice are explicit about professional conduct, behind them are also implicit expectations regarding the conduct of the subjects of professional attention. So, in the doctor–patient relationship, the patient is expected to want to be well, to eat healthily, take exercise and desist from smoking, drug-taking and drinking alcohol. There is an expectation that citizens will actively enhance their life opportunities in ways that also benefit society economically, for example, through engaging in paid work and through parenting that respects and values the educational system and encourages children to do the same. In other words, professional attention is pointed towards developing responsibility on the part of the citizenry, and helping people when things go wrong is in relation to this societal aspiration for social self-regulation and social control. These professional–subject relations embody ethical positioning, and what it is to be a 'good' doctor, lawyer, teacher, social worker, health practitioner is wrapped up in the extent to which the professional is successful in relating to professional subjects in ways that achieve these deontic ends.

The reality of professional experience, of course, is frequently rather different from the above idealised notion of public service. Frequently, teachers, social workers, health practitioners do not know what to do, are riven with conflict arising from dealing with individuals who are not self-regulating, individuals who resist being cured, employed, educated, improved, whatever. Professionals in the public services address these situations through professional judgement. In writing about youth workers, Bradford (2007), drawing on Foucault's concept of ethics in which individual experience and reflection are central (Davidson, 1994), explains that becoming a 'good' youth worker requires work on the self as well as direct work with youth. It is this self-reflection that distinguishes the professional from the volunteer, not autonomous action, for 'modern aspirant professionals (like youth workers) work in bureaucracies in which their work is substantially controlled by administrators' (Bradford, 2007: 294).

Reflection as an attribute is integrated into professional training, and is supposed to provide the means by which the professional person can help themselves to work in alternative ways. Nonetheless, stress levels in public service professionals are high as people try to make sense of difficult and sometimes tragic situations in the glare of public attention, aware that, should they be unsuccessful, the code of practice governing their activities has the power to render them 'unprofessional' and possibly 'unfit to practise'.

Webster (2010) considers the case of the Social Care Code of Practice in the UK, and argues that this, and by implication other codes of practice, have become so dominating as to limit the freedom of thought that genuine reflection entails.

Nevertheless it is through being subject to the challenges inherent in professional life that may lead the person to research in the first place, as research becomes the means by which the professional explores and thinks about tensions between the ideal practice and the actual. Research writing may also be the way that the person undertakes reflection on practice, the work on self that helps to legitimate a position as a 'good' professional.

Research ethics

Universities have processes and procedures to protect participants and institutions involved in research projects conducted under their name, and these increasingly apply to research conducted by both staff and by students, at undergraduate as well as postgraduate levels. These generally come under the umbrella of ethical guidance provided by research funders or research associations such as the American Education Research Association, the UK Economic and Social Research Council, or the Social Research Association. The protocols are concerned with two specifics: working with health and safety hazards, and working with people either rendered vulnerable through the research or considered to be less autonomous or powerful, for example children and young people, or people with mental or physical health problems. These ethics protocols also serve to protect researchers from working in dangerous situations. The requirement that research is ethically cleared by the university offers some protection from redress should things go wrong. Professions in which research is undertaken also normally require ethical clearance before any project is given permission to proceed. Health professionals and social work professionals usually have to submit an application for clearance, and for doctoral researchers this often means complying with more than one set of procedures, which can take time.

In classical moral decision-making terms, these approaches to research ethics are consequentalist and utilitarian. Guidelines for research ethics may seem rationalised, impersonal, bureaucratic constructions that are not conducive to handling context-specific, value- and emotion-laden decisions of individuals and groups at a particular time and place. Ethical checks and balances are front-ended, setting out researcher intentions. Such front-ended processes tend to assume research that is more predictable. However, for social scientists, what appear to be the issues at the beginning of the project are rarely all that there is to it, and so ethical clearance at that stage is unlikely to cover what actually happens over the course of the study. In sum, ethical research procedures are designed so that researchers anticipate ethical issues arising from their research before the project begins and consider these carefully, and at the outset of a research project, ethical protocols can help researchers navigate some complicated ethical conundrums.

Nevertheless, practitioner researchers are quite possibly working within a professional practice in which values of duty are embedded, and are seeking to explore that practice from an ethical position that is predicated on there being consequences of each and every research decision. Adopting these positions means remaining involved with possibly several ethical stances simultaneously, all of which must be managed with integrity. Usher (2000) argues that this requires a different concept of ethics than that offered by modernist epistemology – predominantly one that recognises that subjectivity is created out of the conditions of the context, as well as the people within it.

By understanding that subjectivities and moral voices are made up from the cultural, social and historical settings in which the insider research is conducted, we understand that ethical guidelines cannot on their own anticipate the diversity of all the lives of those involved in research studies.

Situational ethics and complications for insider researchers

It is not difficult to envisage some of the ethical dilemmas inherent in these positions. Working and researching in the same establishment gives practitioner doctoral researchers potentially easy access to their participants and both the researcher and the researched must live with this. There are inevitably also potential tensions through the researcher's relations with colleagues. Thus difficulties may arise through potential exploitation of close personal and professional relationships, and authority over junior staff and/or students. These include, for example, the potential for raising suspicion amongst participants about the purpose of the study and the consequences of being identified with 'negative' or 'uncomfortable' findings, the possibility of 'hidden agendas' and assurance that confidentiality will be maintained. For example, a teacher identifying through research what they perceive to be unsound practice may be accused, by managers and peers, of being unprofessional or uncollegial. They may perhaps even feel unable to share their views. When an insider or action researcher comes across work-based unethical behaviour disclosed by someone who is being interviewed or observed, for instance learning about someone's dishonesty (say, for example, stealing from a client), what does the researcher do? Let it pass? More subtly, suppose a researcher encounters sexism, homophobia or racism beneath a veneer of respectability. We referred in Chapter 3 to the apologia from Ozga and Gewirtz (1994) who actively played on organisational sexism in order to gain access to elite members of the civil service. Under what circumstances might 'getting your moral hands dirty' either by condonement or collusion be justified? Whistle-blowing is a key ethical consideration for any practitioner researcher and is actually required of a registered social worker.

Other concerns surround the perception of some participants that there might be a hidden and unspoken benefit for them in agreeing to take part in the research. For instance, one university undergraduate described as 'surprising' his 40 per cent assignment mark which he thought should have been higher because he had 'helped' the lecturer by taking part in his research. Guidelines are usually explicit in stating that researchers must not privilege any participants over others through the study, for example, the British Education Research Association (BERA, 2004: 8) states 'researchers must take steps to minimize the effects of designs that advantage, or are perceived to advantage one group of participants over others'. However, such perceptions may not be obvious to the early career researcher until after the study is completed.

Kelly asks 'how does one write an honest but critical report if one hopes to continue to work with those involved?' She concludes that the insider researcher's position 'lies uncomfortably between that of the internal evaluator whose main loyalty is to colleagues and the organisation and the external researcher for whom informal comments and small incidents may provide the most revealing data' (1989: 63), However, as Doucet and Mauthner (2008) argue, relationships with participants cannot necessarily take precedence over other relationships and commitments, including those people and communities who will read, use and build on the research findings. Therefore, ethical issues need to be framed and considered in terms of the wider relationships that go beyond those with colleagues and friends.

Practitioners conducting insider research also have to consider issues arising from digital technologies and virtual networks which have led to new modes of communication, dissemination and publication. Using these ethically needs thought, for the insider researcher is able to work collegially in a digital setting which leaves traces of what has been said by whom to whom (Qin et al., 2000).

If participants believe themselves and/or their views to be 'betrayed', even if this is not the researcher's perspective, then continuing professional and personal relationships at work and outside may be damaged. Betrayal of trust is also connected with an abuse of power, and descriptions of situations in which people feel betrayed also always include some dimension of power relations. In our study, we met Jonathan, a secondary school headteacher whose doctoral study had included talking to school pupils about their experience of mathematics teaching in his school. What the students revealed was then reflected to the teachers in the mathematics department, in order to provoke them to change their teaching approaches. Some of the teachers expressed that they had been betrayed by the powerful headteacher speaking behind their backs about their work with pupils. In this case, Jonathan used his rank to access information that he intended to use professionally (and dutifully) in powerful ways, which of course as headteacher he was entitled to do. However, a more experienced researcher might have predicted that resistance was likely to occur on the part of the mathematics teachers when confronted by direct criticism, and might well have approached the issues differently so as to keep the teachers onside, both with the research and with the anticipated professional development. As it was, Jonathan left the school for another post in order to distance himself from the sources of his data whilst he was writing up his thesis. Another instance came from an EdD researcher, also a university lecturer in teacher education, whose line manager, doing a masters degree, asked to 'borrow' her literature review relating to a particular project so as to include it in his own account of that same project. In this second case, the betrayal arose from the high-status professional taking advantage of rank to claim research work that he had not done as his own. Newkirk (1996) warns of qualitative approaches possibly resulting in acts of seduction, ending in betrayal as participants are reconstructed in the final text to meet the researcher's agenda. This potential for seduction and betrayal is greater when the researcher is an insider and a professional in the participant community. Such friendly 'conversations' may not represent what is reconstructed and interpreted as research data and may not sit well with the participants' sense of self (Stronach & MacLure, 1997). This means that the researcher has to tread a fine line. The researchers must continue to engage with the processes and practices of the institution in which they work whilst at the same time potentially being critical of them. Thus there is the constant struggle to develop a critical research stance whilst at the same time maintaining allegiance to the institution and to colleagues who may be participants in a study.

To conduct research in which colleagues are participants is to accept that attention must be paid to the power relations as well as the social relations between colleagues; that these relations are complex and potentially include elements of coaxing, persuading, pushing, pressurising and other forms of influence that outsider researchers would not be able to wield (Miles & Huberman, 1994). Furthermore, it is much more difficult to preserve anonymity, either of the institution from the outside world, or of the participants from each other. Research in the workplace is likely to be on a small scale and involve few people. And it is not easy to 'lose' people in a small 'qualitative crowd' (Hammersley & Atkinson, 1983: 209). Does this mean that insider research is inevitably unethical? We believe not at all, but that decisions regarding research activity will necessarily build upon ethical dimensions that must be taken into account at every stage, continually, negotiated and re-negotiated with reference to participants, power relations, professional practice and institutional politics. As a result, as well as observing ethical codes of practice and for research, practitioner researchers at doctoral level will become ethical as they wrestle with the dilemmas and contradictions that emerge from researching in this manner.

One of the ways in which we might think about ethical 'being' has resurfaced from Aristotle's concept of virtue ethics in Macfarlane's (2008) version of ethical behaviour, an approach that places researchers centrally as responsible for the conduct of the project from the initial conception of ideas through to dissemination. How do insider researchers manage all of these responsibilities in practice in ethical ways? Macfarlane suggests 'self-regulation' which will include making professional as well as research judgements and acknowledging conflict and tensions between these. Foucault seeks to understand social dynamics of ethics as an 'ontological space in which subject does detailed reflexive work on self' (Foucault, quoted in Bradford, 2007: 305). There may also be professional requirements that govern the conduct of research, for example, in the UK it is as necessary for researchers in schools as it is for teachers to have been cleared as not having criminal convictions. Practitioners conducting insider research at doctoral level must integrate the demands of academia, of researching, of new technology and of increased accountability, whilst at the same time maintaining and improving their own professional practice. All of these areas have their own demands and sometimes their own codes, cultures and practices can be in conflict (Gorman, 2007: 8).

Furthermore, there are many differences in relationships between academics and practitioners in terms of setting of the research agenda, the policy implications that may flow from it and the right to publish outcomes. Each may be governed by research ethics standards which may not always be compatible or serve the mutual interests of both parties (Campbell & Groundwater-Smith, 2007: 2). We found in our study that insider doctoral researchers found ways of negotiating and re-negotiating relationships with their colleagues. Hammersley and Atkinson point out that for insider researcherss being: 'Allowed to play are a matter of negotiation and re-negotiation between the self and others in a context of shifting power relations. This is affected as much by the setting as by ideological, methodological and personal factors' (1983: 76). There are good and bad negotiators and the process of negotiation to a greater or lesser extent depends on their power to persuade.

Phronesis helps researchers develop principles of good sense to help decide how to proceed. Flyvbjerg (2001) suggests that in social science researchers tend to address the following four value-rational questions to guide decisions about taking action:

- Where are we going?
- Is this development desirable?
- Who gains and who loses, and by which mechanisms of power?
- What, if anything, should we do about it?

This approach continues throughout the work, for as the project develops, the more tensions between the professional environment and the imperatives of the research are likely to emerge. In asking these questions, the researcher continues to explore his or her position with respect to the dominance of the work in relation to the participants in the study, and so does work on self that makes the project ethically reflexive. This is an important element of the reflexive methodology discussed in Chapter 4, suggesting that the research endeavour in itself is an ethical exploration. Ethically sound research involves values and judgements that bring together the academic, the professional and the personal, and are coded as: trust/truthfulness/honesty; integrity; respect; impartiality and fairness; accuracy; openness; and reflexive awareness. These interactions lead to complex and context-dependent ethical positions.

The concept of an ethics that is situated is also 'attractive to feminists because it is central to their concerns about hegemonic, epistemological and moral traditions which define who and what may make a claim to truth and moral knowledge' (Simons & Usher, 2000). They argue that diverse moral voices have been marginalised and, in some cases, silenced, and that a more discursive approach is required to represent a more inclusive ethical approach. Thus, value ethics operated in a plurality of places and situated in local contexts takes account of a more diverse lived experience.

Ethical relativism and versions of cultural or ethnocentric traditions versus some absolute ethical standard are always being weighed against each other. If a researcher comes across immorality (however defined) it is up to them to decide what to do about it and at what point. This requires a tacit intuitive feel and adroitness required for understanding, interpreting and dealing with fluid evolving situations and an emerging research context, whilst remaining ethical. It is suggested (e.g. Peterson & Seligman, 2004) that there are some specific global trans-cultural virtues that can be identified with a morally attuned researcher character under the banner virtue 'wisdom and knowledge'. This cluster entails creativity, curiosity, open-mindedness, love of learning, perspective, all combined with other virtues of justice, courage, humanity, temperance and transcendence.

This relative situated position of the researcher in the research setting does not sit easily with efforts to explain dilemmas in terms of role conflict between practitioner and researcher. For example, Stacey (1988) claims that betrayal of trust is recognised as a potential outcome of multiple 'roles', and Gorman (2007) asserts that in all practice-based research, complications can arise if there are conflicts between researcher 'roles' and practitioner 'responsibilities'. Doctoral training for insider researchers to start with may ask participants to explicitly address how being a practitioner and being a researcher differ. However, as Hajer (1995) explains, the idea of 'role' implies that people can separate their actions according to different functions, and indeed we are used to people beginning a sentence with phrases such as 'with my ... hat on', or 'speaking as a...'. In considering insider-research, the very term 'insider' implies a boundary with the default being 'outsider' research. But there is no such thing. There is no disinterested researcher. As the project proceeds, there is a merging of these functions so that both research and practice inform each other. This reflexivity requires us to let go our grip on the ideas of 'researcher role' or 'practitioner role' and instead to think in terms of position. The ethical practitioner researcher must 'intuit thoughtfully' when big virtues like justice and humanity might need to trump the virtues of research in the pursuit of new knowledge.

Chapter 6

What does doctoral pedagogy bring to practitioner research?

Increasingly, doctoral training in the UK is tending towards the model established in North America and Australia, where doctoral researchers progress through taught elements before embarking on the main thesis. These elements usually consist of some face-to-face group meetings, some individual tutorial or supervision sessions and using a virtual learning environment such as WebCT, BlackBoard or Moodle to engage students in discussion between face-to-face events. Usually, this taught aspect is framed as 'research training'. However, what this means varies considerably, and (Taylor, 2007) points to doctoral pedagogy being fraught with confusion. She identifies considerable diversity between tutor-led practice variously aiming to model research for students to mimic and approaches that intend doctoral researchers to learn from their experience of undertaking research; these various practices are all underpinned by an expectation that the doctoral researcher learns to integrate research with their own individual situation. Often, professional doctorate programmes consist of a period working with a cohort, attending workshops and seminars, followed by a period working individually on a research project. This second phase would normally be 'supervised' by a qualified member of staff through arrangements with the awarding university. The person on the earlier phase may also be supervised, but this also varies from institution to institution.

In this chapter we argue that doctoral pedagogy is inextricably connected to ideologies of what it is understood to mean to undertake a doctoral degree. Thus, given that the development of practitioner research degrees has been haphazard and idiosyncratic, as explained in Chapter 2, it is not surprising that pedagogies for professional doctorates are also confused. This means that doctoral pedagogy can mean different things to readers, doctoral researchers, tutors and supervisors, and those who act as gatekeepers for the research degree such as examiners.

We build on the position that insider doctoral research is undertaken successfully by those who are able to connect with and through relations between higher education practices, that is, research practices, academic practices and practices of teaching and learning. From this stance we explore the place of taught elements in the context of emerging doctoral researcher identity. We argue that it is through two things – expanded learning at work and feedback on writing – from which the doctoral researcher learns the most, and so taught elements are useful to the extent that they provide the opportunity for the practitioner researcher to undertake some work that will generate feedback at doctoral level.

Completing a practitioner doctorate through insider research means locating the workplace as the site of learning about research, and positioning oneself reflexively when undertaking doctoral 'work' with respect to all the domains in which this occurs. This means letting go of the idea of researcher and practitioner 'roles' for, as has been remarked, the idea of role 'assumes that a person is always separable from the role taken up' (Hajer, 1995: 53); and here we see that in fact the person cannot become separable from either researcher or practitioner, for each affects the other. We have suggested elsewhere in this volume (Chapter 8) that the impact of undertaking insider research at doctoral level is more on the person undertaking the research than on their workplace per se, and understanding the relations between the reflexive project and the workplace helps us to see why this might be.

The practitioner researcher needs to negotiate the practices of higher education as part of the reflexive project. Reflexivity means recognising the part one plays in the research process, and as the research is judged by higher education this requires developing a sense of research-informed position. Because the insider project is conducted in the context of professional practice, this position must be with respect to the workplace. Professional norms help shape the position of practitioners with respect to practice – for example, teachers are required to teach the national curriculum, social workers must adhere to the Social Work and Social Care Guidelines, medical practitioners adhere to the Hippocratic Oath and so on. Thus any research undertaken by professionals in their field is shaped by these professional norms, and it is quite impossible for practitioners to stand outside them. This positioning gives a degree of subjectivity to research. Actually it has been named 'subjective-objectivity' in the field of journalism, (for example Donsbach & Klett, 1993), and means recognising that one's professional self, the subject, is presenting a story or account in terms that, however fairly presented or impartial, is governed by this subjective position.

This position has implications for pedagogy as the doctorate can from this standpoint no longer be considered to be 'taught' in the sense of doctoral material being provided and on which the doctoral researchers can be assessed as having 'learned'.

Researcher identity

One way of thinking about doctoral pedagogy might be through identifying a set of learning outcomes that each doctoral researcher should know about. For social scientists these might include thinking about research design and strategy; developing capability in research methods; managing data; developing an epistemological understanding of theorising and how this relates to analysis. When the researcher is also conducting research as an insider into their area of practice, the practice is inextricably entwined with understanding design, methods and data and how it is all theorised and presented as an argument.

In discussing how learning and the context of and for learning are connected, we ascribe to the notion (Edwards & Miller, 2007) that context is 'no longer considered as a container, but as a relational effect' (2007: 263). Work on situated learning (Lave, 1988) shows that the situation is not merely a location for the learner, but is an inextricable aspect of socio-cognition. In other words, applying these ideas at doctoral level suggests that the practice in which the researcher works adds specificity to understanding how research works, and that these understandings of both practice and research cannot be disengaged. Practitioner doctoral students are operating in spaces created through the interaction of several 'contexts' which inevitably interact with each other. This means that the insider researcher develops fluidity with respect to their stance regarding research and practice, with the thesis emerging from an account of position that arises when the researcher and practitioner positions merge.

Activity theory (Engeström, 2001), whereby learners are considered in terms of who they are and, significantly, where they are, helps us to navigate these positions in the case of individuals, and we frame our analysis accordingly in these terms. We draw upon ideas about learning at work (Eraut, 2004a, 2004b) to explore relations between taught aspects of the programme and informal learning undertaken by professional doctorate students, and we consider the relational effects of assessment in helping to shape doctoral researcher identity (Crossouard, 2008; Crossouard & Pryor, 2008; Pryor & Crossouard, 2008).

From this place we question how taught elements relate to the context of emerging doctoral researcher identity. Our premise is that as the ultimate goal of the doctoral researcher is to produce new knowledge, that goal will shape the teaching that helps the researcher develop. Of course new knowledge is rarely predictable in advance, and so what is important is to maximise understanding of what creating new knowledge is likely to mean for the researcher, and for the insider researcher this will be in relation to the awarding university, as well as being in relation to the researcher's workplace.

Figure 6.1 shows three loci of insider doctoral research: the university, the workplace and the reflexive self. It is in the intersections and spaces between these elements that the doctoral researcher must make sense. The thesis must present the research in conventional terms: literature review, methodology, data analysis and discussion and so forth. The substantive area in focus is in the workplace or the community of practice of professional activity. But there is potential for researcher insiderness to compromise the validity of the research, and this creates a risk that needs to be managed. In Chapter 4 we discussed how reflexively locating oneself as an insider in the research process provides a means of establishing authenticity and veracity, and in Chapter 5 we asserted that this has ethical repercussions also. The researcher's reflexive consideration of their position is a significant strand of the project as well as being evident in the thesis.

This set of engagements for the insider researcher, relations between work and developing researcher identity are critical, as is the third dimension, that of the higher education practices through which the doctoral degree is constructed and completed. It is through the higher education institution that the doctoral research is turned into a doctoral degree, with all the attendant criteria implied by this brought to bear. Universities are required to demonstrate confidence in their own and others' comparable products, and currently, in the UK and Australia, must adhere to various 'quality' criteria. It is here that the degree is assessed, and it is through mediating academic practices in relation to their own projects that the candidate writes a thesis that is deemed to be doctoral.

So, in order to address the question of what doctoral pedagogy is setting out to achieve, we should examine what doing a doctorate means for someone engaging in insider research and who is therefore subject to

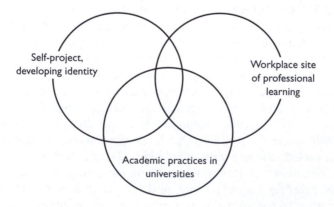

Figure 6.1 Location of practitioner knowledge at doctoral level.

the relations between self, workplace and the higher education practices presented above. We explore the ideas of constructing new knowledge, and how this becomes an individual experience in the circumstance. We explore how learning at work intersects with higher education practices and with an individual's professional experience; and we conclude by bringing these ideas together to establish a purpose for pedagogy.

Expanded learning and constructing new knowledge

Activity theory provides a theory by which learning can be understood in terms of not simply the acquisition of new understandings, skills and knowledge by a person, but also that the interaction of that person with practices for learning in itself also creates new knowledge. Engeström (2001) makes a case for 'expansive learning at work' for situations when professionals engage with problem-solving in workplace settings. We use these ideas of learning to understand what the creation of new knowledge might mean for the insider researcher.

Activity theory is an evolutionary theory that takes account of a socio-cultural set of practices associated with learning following developing ideas of cognition and social theory emanating particularly from northern Europe and Russia throughout the twentieth century. These powerful theories about human thinking and human behaviour arose out of industrialisation, out of desire to understand how knowledge is created and how knowledge can be harnessed to industrial and economic productivity (Engeström, 1996).

The idea of mediation (Vygotsky, 1978) explains that a stimulus for learning and the response, i.e. learning, was transcended by 'a complex, mediated act' engaging learner, teacher, others, what is being learned and the circumstances under which learning is taking place. Vygotsky suggested that critically these interactions involve language, which therefore becomes a significant and necessary element of learning. Using language inevitably draws attention to the social, and so Engeström notes that 'The individual could no longer be understood without his or her cultural means; and the society could no longer be understood without the agency of individuals who use and produce artifacts' (2001: 2). This takes the concept of activity forwards as the focus shifts to complex interrelations between the individual subject and his or her community. So whilst each participant may have overall personal goals for participating in an activity, these are not necessarily congruent with what the participant actually does during it. This theory was developed in a particular time in twentieth-century European history when interest was in controlling mass social movements. This becomes a problematic means of theorising learning when the cultural situation changes, for diversity brings new perspectives to learning that presents a challenge to a social, but monolithic model.

A third level of activity theory takes account of a conceptual need for participants, in engaging with an activity system, to bring and incorporate cultural perspectives and in so doing, creates further dimensions for the new system. So, for example, in the case of a teacher-researcher in a classroom, the presentation of the lesson, the researcher perspective on the lesson and the students' responses to it would engender what has been named the 'third space' (Gutierrez *et al.*, 1999), that is, what is created as a result of dialogue between teacher, researcher and students and their respective cultural positions. Rather than a single system, this conception requires us to think of dialogue between and within actors relating against a backdrop of networks. With this conception, 'the object of activity is a moving target, not reducible to conscious short-term goals' (Engeström, 2001: 4)

Engeström suggests five principles that characterise activity systems. First there is an overall collective purpose to the system. So, considering qualifications, in universities it is the overall provision of these that is the most important thing. However, the pursuit of qualifications is not necessarily the primary object of the workplace in which the researcher is located (although, for example, in schools, collecting qualifications may act as a proxy for the primary purpose of teaching the curriculum). The goals of individuals and sub-groups can be understood only when interpreted against the background of entire activity systems. Second, there are always multiple points of view, traditions and interests in an activity system and the participants each carry their own histories. The way that work is divided arises from understanding these diverse histories and the activity system itself carries multiple layers and strands of history engraved in its artefacts, rules and conventions. Third, activity systems take shape and are transformed over lengthy periods of time, and so problems in activity systems and the potential for change can only be understood against the backdrop of their own history. Fourth, contradictions are historically accumulating structural tensions within and between activity systems, and are sources of change and development because, in generating disturbances and conflicts, they also generate attempts to change the activity. Finally, we are reminded that changing an activity system takes rather a long time, occurring as a result of individuals who question established norms as contradictions become more evident. Sometimes this escalates into collaborative envisioning and a deliberate collective change effort. This approach has a basis in organisational theory (Tolbert & Zucker, 1996) with the argument that energies spent on changing institutions per se result in strategic compliance without any necessarily real change in practices. On the other hand, a focus on individuals developing practices within organisations reveals change that happens in stages over a period of time. Individuals innovate new ways of working, often in response to external drivers, that then become more widespread in the organisation until decision-makers acknowledge and agree the value of the new approach. Once this endorsement is given, the processes then become embedded in the practices of the organisation.

Practitioner researchers working for a doctoral degree are operating in at least two activity systems, one being the workplace, the other being the awarding university. Considering the awarding university, someone undertaking a doctoral degree through practitioner research as a 'learner' and the object of the activity system 'the provision of doctoral degrees', we can understand the twin individual goals of both undertaking practitioner research and obtaining a doctoral degree as subordinate to the overall proliferation of practitioner research degrees (discussed in Chapter 2). Seen through this lens, the individual's experience of doing such a doctorate may be positioned with respect to this backdrop in terms of who and where they are; why they are making the effort to learn; what is being learned, what are the contents and outcomes of learning; and how the person learns what are the key actions or processes. Doctoral pedagogy must be constructed to enable the person to operate successfully in this activity system, that is, in the system set up to award doctoral degrees.

However, when the activity system is taken to be the community of practice at work, the doctoral researcher becomes positioned differently in terms of organisational change. Instead of fulfilling the goal of production of doctoral degrees, the insider researcher is now placed at a much earlier stage of organisational change, at the stage of individual changing practices. We discuss this further in Chapter 8, for the impact on the insider researcher of undertaking a doctoral degree is not largely on the workplace per se in visible differences to practice, but on the way the individual thinks about practice. Notwithstanding this, practice over time does change, and contributing to the development of communities of practice are the aims and aspirations of many of the individuals participating in them.

This combination of activity system together with individuals makes sense of Engeström's proposal that, whichever way one looks at it, this combination is unique and knowledge-generating. Engeström calls this new knowledge 'expansive learning at work', and he proposes that it can only be explained in this way, i.e. by considering the participants together with the socio-cultural context. Drawn from observing that learning in organisations violates the presupposition that what is to be learned is stable and defined, he argues that 'people and organisations are all the time learning something that is not stable, not even defined or understood ahead of time' (2001: 5). These learning transformations, important in terms of our personal lives and organisational practices, mean that we must create new forms of learning that are not yet there, new patterns of activity and expansive learning at work actually produces new forms of work. It is this formulation that becomes new knowledge, i.e. the specific relations between the individual, their experience and the practices of doctoral education creates some expanded learning both for the individual and the corpus of doctoral education.

The practitioner researcher undergoing doctoral study does so for a variety of reasons. In her study of supervisor practices one of us (Linda) spoke with people undertaking EdDs about why they were undertaking these projects. Interestingly, in her study no one reported being particularly interested in researching at work per se. Instead, these people mainly talked from two perspectives, which were, first, obtaining a doctorate and, second, in terms of career ambitions. They thought a professional doctorate might be easier (which it was not) because it would be structured in such a way as to provide shared experience with other professional doctoral researchers. In terms of ambition, people spoke of enhanced career prospects, obtaining higher qualifications for improved promotion prospects and, in some cases, to prove a point. Wellington and Sikes (2006) write about professional doctorate students who see the doctorate as a chance for reparation of previous educational 'failure', for example the eleven-plus. Other commentators add a work-related dimension, with people expressing a desire to understand problematic aspects of practice, or tensions at work through research, perhaps in the belief that doing research would provide a perspective on these issues that everyday work experience does not. So, for example, a health visitor is keen to promote the interests of 'hard-to-reach groups' (Ebeid, 2008); a medic involved in professional training wants to understand how medical perspectives connect with other professional perspectives when working with less-advantaged groups of people (Hill *et al.*, 2009); and a university administrator hopes to bring an academic voice into matters of quality assurance in the university.

The pathway that is designed for practitioner researchers to tread is geared towards the overall activity of successful completion of doctoral degrees. But the journey that the researcher takes towards that goal is individualised, connected to and dependent on who the person is and why, how and what forms their learning experiences are. This point is important when constructing pedagogy, and we will return to it in the concluding section of this chapter.

Learning and work

For practitioner researchers, there are three forms of 'work' that the doctoral candidate must engage with. There is work, as in professional work. Then there is work as required for the practitioner research degree – normally some demonstration of successful academic practice such as assignments and invariably a research thesis. And finally there is transformative work in the reflexive project – i.e. making sense of it all.

Eraut constructs a continuum of learning at work, with formal at one end and informal at the other, characterising informal learning as 'The informal end of the continuum of formality includes implicit, unintended, opportunistic and unstructured learning and the absence of a teacher' (2004a: 251). He also points out that 'formal education can be also viewed as a workplace and uses a discourse in which the term "work" is normally quite prominent' (2004b: 248). He points out that universities take for granted the significance of learning that happens via their ministrations, but that knowledge acquired elsewhere, for instance in a workplace setting, is of little concern generally in academic programmes. In this work Eraut pulls together a meta-narrative of learning at work drawing on several projects and earlier thinking about tacit knowledge (see, for example, Eraut, 1994). Eraut steers towards considering opportunities for informal learning at work and points out that 'informal learning in formal settings' is an under-researched area. This recent work helps us to theorise 'informal learning' and what this actually might mean for practitioner researchers. Another study (Macrae *et al.*, 2003), of undergraduate mathematics students, showed that success was very much connected with who the students lived with, their friends, their paid work, their ability to make contact with tutors and to get feedback. In the case of postgraduate researchers, practitioners who set up and use learning opportunities, for example initiating personal discussion with tutors or friendships with other doctoral researchers, perhaps via social networking websites such as Facebook (Chandler-Grevatt *et al.*, 2008), are engaging in informal learning, although as Eraut argues that these opportunities for informal learning come from interaction with successful learners, there are attendant risks. Doctoral researchers should establish peer reference groups with care, and the extent to which higher education explicitly facilitates these informal but crucial forms of support for learning is an important dimension to navigating the academic practice required for doctoral study.

Learning at work, suggests Eraut, depends almost entirely on the context in which the person is operating, their previous experience and their future behaviour; as Melvyn Bragg argued (2008), we are all operating in the past, the present and the future all at the same time – that is what making sense of experience is all about. The point, Eraut suggests, is that much if not all of the learning that people do at work is situated in that work, and is informal. Thus, transferring knowledge from a higher education discourse to the workplace is 'much more complex than commonly perceived' (2004a: 256). When discussing learning from other people, Eraut writes:

> People who work in both contexts have to be bilingual, but this does not mean that they become good interpreters. Knowledge of how to use formal knowledge from higher education settings in practice contexts has a very strong tacit dimension; and this affects how it can be learned.
>
> (2007: 404)

What does learning to do research entail?

Creating new knowledge suggests new pedagogy, assessment and legitimating of different forms of knowledge. Thorne (2001) provides a starting point for thinking about pedagogy by categorising into four types the motivations of different people on three different programmes, the Doctorate in Business Administration, the Doctorate in Education and the Doctorate in Engineering. A typology was developed from interviews with students which enabled comparison between the different programmes; the identified types are: Type One, 'extrinsic-professional initiation'; Type Two, 'extrinsic-professional continuation'; Type Three, 'extrinsic-professional alteration'; and Type Four, 'intrinsic-personal/professional affirmation'. Type One is characterised by students who identify their doctorate directly with career development; Type Two is characterised by students who are senior professionals and who wish to further develop their professional career or find new opportunities through diversifying career options; Type Three describes students who use the doctorate as a vehicle for changing an aspect of their own practice; whilst Type Four is characterised by students who pursue the doctorate for its own sake, or with an intrinsic interest in the subject matter and/or the process of doctoral study. Considering these may be helpful in ascribing motivation to doctoral researchers as it may help in identifying 'who are the learners, and what, why and how do they learn?'

Becoming a researcher involves learning and practising technical skills as well as the more sophisticated integration of learning how to relate research, higher education and work. The Research Councils in the UK welcome professional doctorate programmes on the grounds that, being grounded in application, there are direct opportunities for practitioners to apply academic knowledge. Generally concerned about the provision of research training, these research councils have constructed a set of requirements which aim to give a 'common view of the skills and experience of a typical research student' (in Lunt, 2002). These requirements for research students include providing: training in research skills and techniques; a research environment and skills in research management, personal effectiveness and communication; opportunities for networking and team working; and preparation in career management.

This gives curriculum designers something to get hold of, and the extent to which each set of experiences may be helpful or relevant for differing groups of doctoral researchers can be considered, perhaps in terms of the Thorne typology described above. However, this will only be a starting point, for whilst it may be the case that in general there are distinctive features of doctoral researchers on different doctoral degrees, be these professional and applied, putting people into pedagogical groupings does not help in identifying the new learning that emerges from the particular combination of individual, workplace and research situation, and engaging with higher education practices for individuals in those groups. This may be annoying for organisers of curricula in doctoral programmes who want to provide a generality of experience that can be taught, but there it is, a consequence of the need for doctoral level work to be original.

However, this begs the question of how the transformation of the professional practitioner into doctoral researching practitioner occurs and so we must sidle up to pedagogy in a further way. Pedagogy relates to all the work that the doctoral researcher undertakes in making sense of the higher education practices that will ultimately lead to the degree. For this to happen, researchers' written work will be regularly assessed, with formative feedback becoming an important aspect of the pedagogic relationships between them and the providing university. Eventually as the doctoral researcher moves to working only with a supervisor on the thesis, this feedback becomes the sole means of pedagogic relations. Arguably, any taught elements of the doctoral programme serve simply to ensure that the researcher produces some writing that can be assessed at doctoral level. It is the job of the researcher to make sense of this feedback, for in so doing they will be engaging successfully with the necessary academic practices. Crossouard and Pryor make this point forcefully, arguing that doctorates now necessarily need interventionist pedagogic strategies because cultural norms of the lone researcher doing their own thing can no longer be assumed to apply.

> With a larger and more diverse doctoral intake, non-intervention may disempower students who do not share the gendered, classed and ethnic norms implicit within academic cultures (Johnson et al. 2000). Given the changing doctoral intake, the arguments that doctoral supervision should be reconceptualised as a pedagogic relationship are therefore strong.
>
> (2008: 226)

Whilst some practitioners accept being positioned as a student as an inevitable aspect of their new position as learners in higher education, others are more discomfited. Malfroy (2005) conducted a study of two professionally oriented doctoral programmes, one a PhD in Environmental Health, Tourism and Management and the other a Professional Doctorate programme in Nursing and Midwifery. Whilst the professional doctorate group appreciated the collegiality of their programme, professionals in the group pointed to 'student–supervisor' labelling of relations as emphasising an unequal hierarchy; and supervisors of the same people commented also on the need to learn 'side-by-side' because of the practice dimension about which they knew little. We develop this discussion of supervision in Chapter 7.

We began this chapter by drawing attention to lack of clarity about doctoral pedagogy. We conclude the chapter having drawn attention to important aspects of becoming a successful doctoral researcher, in other words, significant vectors in the doctoral learning experience. This most importantly includes developing a reflexive self to help in relating higher education and professional practice, and brings the uniqueness that will warrant the work being original. In finding this place, each individual will avail themselves to a greater or lesser extent with the taught programme, with doctoral experience development provided by the university, with informal opportunities to connect with peers, and with their supervisor. Seen in this way implies that the doctoral pedagogy serves to enable the doctoral researcher to achieve expanded learning, and that the means by which this occurs is through the negotiation of the doctoral discourse via engagement with doctoral writing by researchers and tutors alongside self-conscious awareness of practice norms and researching in this space. Feedback therefore becomes the most important means of transmission of higher education norms and expectations. Feedback between peers is also the means by which the integration of practice is articulated. The provision of feedback must be considered to be the single most important aspect of doctoral pedagogy, and it is through feedback that the practitioner researcher integrates the professional knowledge that they understand, but the supervisor may not, with new understandings regarding academic practices.

Chapter 7

The shaping of doctoral knowledge and supervision

In this chapter we explore relationships between how doctoral knowledge is created and the main form of teaching, which at the thesis stage is through supervision from a doctoral supervisor. Doctorates are many and various, and it is not unreasonable to suppose that doctorates designed for different purposes may be supervised differently from each other. Indeed, the United Kingdom Council for Graduate Education is promoting the notion of doctoral differences in a series of meetings and conferences (UKCGE, 2008, 2009) aimed so that those involved in providing doctoral education can think carefully about issues inherent in contemporary doctoral education.

Supervising practitioner research at doctoral level can bring specific challenges, most clearly derived from controversy regarding forms of knowledge. Supervisory relationships between tutors and doctoral researchers have special distinguishing ideals for insider researchers creating professional knowledge. We explore what 'new' knowledge is produced through practitioner research, especially through a professional doctorate, and what it may look like, and discuss what is inescapably central for practitioner researchers at doctoral level: the alignment of professional and academic knowledge.

There are problems associated with discussing the professional doctorate at all. Programmes are currently institution-specific and thus are not a homogeneous group sharing a key set of attributes but rather a widely differing group of individually designed and bespoke programmes each attempting to draw particular target groups. Currently many people undertake insider and/or practitioner research that leads to the PhD. So, any proposals that attempt to uncover and critically analyse conceptions of professional doctorate supervision in relation to knowledge about practice must also acknowledge the lack of analytical unity of the classification of 'professional doctorate' (Scott *et al.*, 2004: 99). However, as much of the work regarding the contribution of practitioners' doctoral work to professional knowledge creation is in the context of professional doctorates, these degrees are the starting point for this discussion.

There may be distinctive aspects of supervising someone undertaking insider research for a professional doctorate that are not evident with insider research for a PhD, as a central tenet of many professional doctorates is the need to integrate 'academic' or propositional knowledge and 'professional' or experiential knowledge. Discussion that involves integration of different types of knowledge needs first to consider whether different types of knowledge can indeed be identified, and if so, how. Then it may be possible to point to differences between them. We take as a starting point the model of Gibbons *et al.* that distinguishes between Mode One and Mode Two knowledge, and then show that accepting this model to analyse process and practices of practitioner researchers on a professional doctorate is problematic.

Table 7.1 highlights the differences between Gibbons *et al.*'s (1994) model of Mode One and Mode Two knowledge.

The traditional PhD, originally intended to produce Mode One propositional knowledge, is associated with and defined by academia, with the primary purpose of sustaining the recruitment of academics and contributing ideologically or theoretically to academic fields of knowledge (Thorne, 2001). In contrast, the main aim of the professional doctorate (which may be said to produce Mode Two experiential knowledge) is to make a significant contribution to practice and practitioner knowledge through research (see Myers, 1996; Barnett, 1997; Jacob, 2000; Lee *et al.*, 2000). But there are a number of problems arising with the model of Gibbons *et al.* First, a traditional PhD may already produce knowledge that is trans-disciplinary and multidisciplinary, since this is the nature of the subject area, and the student may also be researching practice. Second, whilst many professional doctorate programmes aim for their graduates to make a contribution to knowledge of practice, there is currently no assessment of this impact, or potential impact, on practice and no involvement of professionals for whom the research may be intended. Thus, whilst knowledge production in these doctorate degrees currently may take a new form of a critical reflection on working knowledge, it continues to position that knowledge within the academy.

Aligning of academic and professional knowledge

In consideration of professional doctorates it is important to examine the nature of knowledge production (Brew, 2001; Maxwell & Shanahan, 1997). The ways in which the status of professional doctorates is understood, particularly within and outside the academy, is inevitably bound up with questions of perceptions of what counts as valid knowledge. Distinctions between practical knowledge and scholarly knowledge and how these connect with the social world offer an explicit

Table 7.1 Characteristics of Mode One and Mode Two knowledge

Mode One knowledge	Mode Two knowledge
Knowledge that is produced and tested in the academy by researchers	Knowledge that is created and tested by practitioners outside the academy
Disciplinary knowledge	Trans-disciplinary knowledge
Knowing through contemplation	Knowing through action
Knowledge for its own sake	Working knowledge
Knowing 'that'	Knowing 'how'
Knower as spectator	Knower as agent
Propositional knowledge	Knowledge as reflection on practice
Theoretical knowledge	Practical knowledge
Knowledge about the world	Knowledge in the world

Source: Based on Bourner *et al.* (2001); Gibbons *et al.* (1994).

dimension to how we live our lives and what we value as important (Bourdieu, 1997; Bernstein, 1999).

In Table 7.1 it is evident that Gibbons *et al.* make a clear distinction between disciplinary knowledge produced inside the academy, and trans-disciplinary knowledge produced outside the university. Disciplinary or Mode One knowledge is described as propositional, linear and causal and reductionist, seeking to solve problems outside the university and determining what is significant in society. Experiential or Mode Two knowledge, on the other hand, is centred on trans-disciplinary knowledge applied to problems within the workplace and arguably describing knowledge structures emerging from applied or practitioner research at doctoral level.

Bringing professional knowledge into the academy and asking for it to be recognised at the highest level poses a threat to the knowledge-producing scholarly purpose of the university, and as Maxwell and Shanahan propose:

> Professional doctorates must raise epistemological questions about the nature and creation of knowledge, the positioning of knowledge and the relations between those who create it, since they signal a move from the classic model in which academic groups or individuals determine what type of knowledge is valid.
>
> (1997: 212)

Thus confusion surrounding professional doctorates signals in part the current confusion about the condition of knowledge in our society. Knowledge residing in the university implies knowledge produced on a site, 'like the polis for Plato, enjoying the epistemic status of the cave' (Delany, 2001: 1). The current situation is that the nature of 'valid' knowledge is being questioned, not only in the academy but in society more generally, and this is leading to a more reflexive role for knowledge (Schön, 1987). These are the conditions in which the professional doctorate has been developed, the conditions under which insider research has gained credibility as a legitimate means of developing new knowledge about practice, and the conditions also in which traditional doctoral degrees are becoming 'professionalised'.

Since professional doctorates are constructed between the university and the workplace it is not unreasonable to expect there to be some challenges for practitioner researchers on them in successfully integrating academic and professional knowledge, both of which are complex and contested.

If we consider it reasonable to suggest that the integration of professional and academic knowledge is at the heart of professional doctoral study, seeking to produce 'situated theory entering into and emerging from, practice' (Usher, 2000: 127; Bourner *et al.*, 2002), then critical to the production of such situated theory is reflexivity, the awareness of the theorist of their unique part in the construction of new knowledge.

Scott *et al.* (2004) suggest that perhaps the integration of academic and professional knowledge on a professional doctorate may be better described as acknowledging the practice setting as the source of reflection, but not as the arena in which theorising takes place. This may be extremely difficult for practitioner researchers at doctoral level who are at the same time part of the practice setting and the academy, both underpinned by context-related production of different types of knowledge. Thus practitioner researchers must deconstruct existing models of professional knowledge and replace them with a critical and analytic reflection on such knowledge resulting in what has been called 'comfortable (or uncomfortable) schizophrenia' (Argyris & Schön, 1978). It is precisely this paradox with which professional doctorate researchers must wrestle which in turn has implications for their supervisors.

Seddon (2001) argues that professional doctorates not only may represent a less paternalistic and hierarchical academic practice but also may signal a move towards more inclusive and respectful acceptance that learning and knowledge production takes place in a variety of contexts, including the academy. But such positions are not necessarily mutually exclusive. Whilst knowledge that does not get used in practice gets 'consigned to cold storage' (Eraut, 1994: 37), any system which separates professional practice from the teaching of propositional knowledge does not acknowledge the relationship between theory and practice. In any event, to reduce the type of knowledge produced is problematic since it is founded on the belief that professional doctorates signal a general move in one direction and, as we have shown earlier, we know this not to be the case. Some professional doctorates are more like traditional PhDs, as, similarly, some PhDs may be moving towards more of a professional doctorate model. Thus, much depends on the research questions and how the researcher goes about researching these.

Lee *et al.* (2000) believe that rather than separating Mode One and Two knowledge, it is necessary to understand the professional doctorate as a vehicle for creating new forms of knowledge. Scott (1995) goes further in creating a model based on Mode Three and Mode Four which is about knowledge-production. Mode Three knowledge is dispositional and trans-disciplinary and designed to bridge the gap by integrating professional and academic knowledge. Mode Four is critical knowledge explicitly or implicitly designed to change practice.

But the situation is more complex than a simplistic dichotomy between academic and professional knowledge. According to a number of studies (e.g. Polyani, 1966; Schön, 1983; Eraut, 1994; Barnett, 1997), there appears to be a range of different knowledges being produced through professional doctorate degrees, each underpinning power relationships which exist between different knowledge frameworks. Indeed, even the classification of knowledge has itself become a contested field: this is an example of 'supercomplexity' (Barnett, 2000) where even the frameworks for analysis have become unstable.

So what are the implications for supervisors and researchers as they come to terms with the many and varied different types of knowledge that may be part of the doctoral degree? My (Linda's 2005) study showed that whilst students wanted a supervisor who was a senior academic, in fact their highest priority was to be assigned a supervisor with professional knowledge (and preferably experience) of their working context.

Supervisors' academic and professional knowledge and experience

Professional doctorate researchers gain confidence in supervisors whose substantive knowledge is in their chosen field, although it is difficult to see how this expectation can always be met, since the choice of research area that leads to the thesis is frequently some time after first enrolling. What is striking is that these emergent practitioner researchers often lack confidence in their supervisor's knowledge and understanding of professional practice. Students often believe strongly that it is important for professional doctorate supervisors to have considerable professional knowledge and experience themselves in order to understand the professional issues with which the student is engaged. This implies that supervisors should be literate in relation to professional knowledge. Brennan (1995) argues that in many respects, supervisors have had to come to terms with the student's professional context and understand what sort of research and research outcomes might most contribute to the student's profession. Insider researchers themselves too are often concerned that their supervisors have significant substantive knowledge of their field as well as knowledge and experience of their professional contexts (e.g. an insider researcher conducting an investigation into mathematics education in their primary school would expect not only a primary mathematics specialist, but someone who also had experience of teaching maths at that level and understanding the context).

My study revealed that expectations and perceptions play a large part in matching researchers and supervisors. Researchers' views of a good match are often not the same as supervisors' views. Once engaged in supervision, experiences vary depending on the supervisor's interpretation of a practitioner doctorate and whether they see it as a specialist form of PhD or a radically different type of doctorate which requires different types of supervision in order to produce an original contribution to knowledge of practice.

Delamont *et al.* (2004) suggest that a supervisor with no direct subject knowledge in their supervisee's research area can turn such a potential problem into a professional development opportunity by reading around the new area and perhaps even attending appropriate courses on the new topic. Such activities not only have the potential to add to the supervisor's personal and professional development but may also present opportunities for new areas of research. However, in the reality of most professional doctorate supervisors' current workloads, it is difficult to see how more could be added. Some supervisors may feel that supervising outside their area of expertise is an opportunity for personal and professional development, whilst others may feel that their lack of familiarity with literatures in unfamiliar areas could result in a less satisfactory experience both for them and for their students.

Perceptions of professional doctorates and impact on supervision

If the value of experiential learning has been accepted by the academy as valid knowledge (Eraut, 1994) – seen partly through the proliferation of professional doctorate programmes – then this might be interpreted not only as the academy's acceptance, but also as society's current recognition of, and emphasis on, its value. However, despite the first professional doctorate beginning in the UK in 1980, in some respects the social construction of the professional doctorate can be described as being still in its infancy and the wide diversity in the aims, content and practices on a professional doctorate may reflect this embryonic stage. Gergen (2001: 120) suggests that such changes are a result of time and conversations, changing what might originally have been 'true' yesterday; to what is 'ideologically suspect' today. Joint meaning-making emerges from dialogue between those in the field. Social reality is then seen as a product of consensus – the way we think and talk about it and the way we explain it to each other (Finn, 1997).

Alongside the social construction of the professional doctorate and its implications for supervision practices, there are also beliefs about the construction of the doctorate and about what sort of knowledge is being developed. This combination impacts hugely on both supervisor and practitioner researcher, and offers a critical challenge to the supervision of any doctorate.

Findings from my (Linda's) study suggest that interpretations of the professional doctorate and professional doctorate supervision are based on individual perceptions of what sort of knowledge the professional doctorate is intended to contribute to. Trying to capture the essence of current models of the professional doctorate using Gibbons *et al.*'s (1994) bifurcated model of Mode One/Mode Two knowledge may be a helpful starting point but it is no more than a starting point given the recent developments and range of models which seek to integrate professional and academic knowledge. Those who value the advancement of knowledge for its own sake or to satisfy human curiosity are likely to have different conceptions from those who value the advancement of knowledge for its practical contribution to the well-being of people. Such differences go to the very heart of the purpose of learning for each individual.

I (Linda) identified significant differences in what counts as valid knowledge amongst those on the same professional doctorate supervision teams in a single institution. Those with their hearts in the production of Mode One knowledge will start with what is 'known' already framed within a theoretical schema and will proceed to a gap in the literature to be filled. Those with their hearts in the production of Mode Two knowledge will start from what is not 'known' already, i.e. the problems that are being experienced and will be reluctant to limit the options to those offered by any particular pre-formed theoretical framework. Thus, the continuation of supervision and assessment practices which are designed to produce and assess Mode One knowledge (Gibbons *et al.*, 1994) may be operating in an ill-fitting framework.

Lave and Wenger's (1991) theory of different 'communities of practice' does not offer any help with this either. 'Communities of practice' implies a common understanding, common practices and the use of a common language: 'For a community of practice to function it needs to develop ways of doing and approaching things that are shared to some significant extent amongst members' (1991: 98). To consider professional doctoral supervision in the context of a community of academic practice, we should expect a consensus developing around both the professional doctorate per se and professional doctorate supervision at least amongst colleagues in particular university departments. However, this was not confirmed by teams of professional doctorate supervisors in my (Linda's) study. Rather, the differences about the purpose and practice of professional doctorates persisted to a significant extent amongst colleagues who worked closely together on the same professional doctorate programmes.

Differences in supervision practices are, to some extent, underpinned by the supervisor's perspective on the validity of new types of knowledge and alternative ways of knowing evident amongst practitioner researchers. The struggle to maintain what each individual sees as 'legitimate knowledge' (Brew, 2001) are inextricably linked to questions of ownership, knowledge and power. Delamont *et al.* (2004) argue that received notions of the nature of knowledge are related to self-preservation and a willingness (or not) to embrace change. Many, positioned by Bourdieu as social beings, would resist such a challenge since the value individuals place on different types of knowledge is closely bound up with an understanding not only of the world around them, but also of themselves and of their position in it. As Bourdieu put it:

> in short, what individuals and groups invest in the particular meaning they give to systems by the use they make of them is infinitely more than their 'interest' in the usual sense of the term; it is their whole social being, everything which defines their own idea of themselves, the primordial, tacit contract whereby they define 'us' as opposed to 'them'.
>
> (2000: 484)

In the diversity of provision, supervisors are positioned by their own beliefs and values regarding academic knowledge. If, as Bourdieu (1988) suggests, we see the university as the locus of a power struggle between academic and professional knowledge, we are likely to want to preserve the status and value of academic knowledge through related content, process, practice and discourse and be less keen to embrace professional knowledge or integrate academic and professional knowledge in new ways of knowing. However, if practitioner research is seen as combining theory with the complex and messy business of professional practice it will be necessary to explore and acknowledge new amalgamations of different types of knowledge.

There may be little current consensus amongst supervisors regarding supervision, implying inconsistency of staff aspirations for student performance within doctoral work undertaken by practitioner researchers, and consequences for assessment that are likely to be at least confusing. There may be some case for different conceptions of the professional doctorate between different universities in terms of the variety of student choice and diversity of student needs but it is difficult to see any advantages to the persistence of different conceptions of the professional doctorate amongst staff *within* each programme.

Significant problems in the supervision of practitioner researchers may arise from different, and ultimately unhelpful, conceptions of the professional doctorate which in turn depend on the value and status different academics place on academic and professional knowledge. When professional doctorates are seen to operate in a similar way to a traditional PhD as during the thesis phase, they each may be said to be reinforcing both the field and habitus of the academy (Bourdieu, 1988). In Bourdieu's terms, the dominant players in the academic field reproduce and reinforce their status and power, through content, process, practice and discourse. This resonates with Bernstein's (1999) discussions of knowledge discourse, with only certain forms, vertical knowledge discourse, transmitted explicitly through pedagogic practices in educational institutions. Other knowledge, horizontal knowledge discourse, is everyday knowledge informal and weakly classified. This means that professional knowledge must somehow be transformed into vertical knowledge discourse in order for it to be recognisable in the academy. This is a new departure, for, as is explained by Gergen, transmission of knowledge from the academy though curriculum makers and planners into practice environments frequently and recognisably happens hierarchically in a top-down manner. More inclusive discourses might be described as moving 'from monologue to dialogue; from hierarchy to heterarchy where others are involved to comment' (2001: 127). The challenge of new ways of knowing being incorporated into academic life is seen in other discourses too – for instance, David (2002) points to feminist knowledge with its greater emphasis on biography, narratives and 'voices' becoming part of the new knowledge economy.

These are some of the problems with which practitioner researchers and supervisors must concern themselves. Alongside the discourses which supervisors and researchers engage in, students must currently aim to write successfully in an academic genre since dissertations are concerned with academic forms of writing. But it is also likely that the researcher hopes their work will reach a wider audience interested in the outcomes of the research, including colleagues in the workplace and professionals in the wider field (Lee *et al.*, 2000; Maxwell *et al.*, 2001), writing for whom will be in a different genre and style. This question is examined in more depth in Chapter 9, as actually the readership of doctoral writing is small unless the material is transformed into a different form.

Barnett questions whether challenges such as this do indeed represent a fundamental change to the university's value background:

> do we have to accept that the academic community is a collection of contrasting language games, each going its own way, with its own view as to what counts as truth, with its own relation to the wider society and with its own sense as to what is important in the development of the individual? ... an educational process can be termed a higher education when the student is carried to levels of reasoning which make possible a critical reflection on his or her experiences, whether consisting of propositional knowledge or of knowledge through action.
>
> (1990: 21–22)

Vested interests in preserving the status quo means that both the academy and professional communities have their own views of the 'real' and the 'good' and both tend towards insulation from anything that lies outside their boundaries (Gergen, 2001: 132). But all forms of knowledge need to be thrown into question, treated as problematic and understood in terms of the political and economic interests that they serve and by which they are reciprocally sustained (Parker, 1997; Finn, 1997; Nightingale & Cromby, 1999).

There are differences in perceptions of how knowledge relates to doctoral research, with respect to questions regarding the original contribution of this work to knowledge creation. There are calls for greater consensus amongst those working on professional doctorate teams (see, for example, UKCGE, 2002), not only in terms of a more common understanding of this knowledge, or range of knowledges, but also in terms of the current potential for widely different experiences for students on different programmes, or indeed within one team in a single institution. The suggestion that new forms of preparation for supervising a practitioner researcher on a professional doctorate might include some form of 'training' is one that we would argue could equally be considered across all forms of practitioner research at doctoral level, and indeed in the UK it is not only recommended that doctoral supervisors to be 'trained' in practitioner doctorate supervision (UKCGE, 2002), but that all supervisors at doctoral level update their skills every three to five years.

Training of supervisors and training for supervisors

Calls for professional doctorate supervisor 'training' reflect instrumentalist interpretations of research education. Manathunga (2002) declares that the development of effective supervisors must relate to more than imparting technical supervisory skills – what room is there, for example, for intuitive pedagogical understanding of effective doctoral supervision? A more rigorous identification of understanding what makes effective supervision at doctoral level might do much to identify suitable areas for training, rather than what she sees as the anecdotal and personal recollections which often drive supervisor training needs.

Training provision may not have kept pace with recent developments and may still be firmly fixed on how to become a supervisor of someone aiming to produce Mode One knowledge, rather than how to become an effective supervisor of practitioner researchers at doctoral level, helping to develop new knowledges that may combine dimensions of Mode One and Mode Two knowledge. Many doctoral supervisory skills are generic, but there are at least differences in the timescale of different types of doctorate, the size and scope of theses, supervising students in the early stages of a professional doctorate and how this differs from the thesis stage and practicalities such as submission deadlines. To that extent, at least, supervision is context-specific.

Moreover, the tact required in suggesting supervision training for experienced PhD supervisors to meet these new forms of practitioner research, and the potential offence that such a suggestion might cause, should not be underestimated:

> you always risk offending ... the question is who do you risk offending if you say everybody needs training? There are some Professors here who would assert that they've been supervising doctoral students for eons ... for twenty or more years and there are things they don't need to learn ... I would disagree with that but it's difficult to disagree.
>
> (Heath, 2005: 305)

Training for supervising the doctorate currently ranges from short one-off workshops to more systematic, ongoing programmes of support. In the former case, the process and content of workshops is developed in isolation from the participants and is generic in nature. In the latter case, which has historically been more widespread in Australian universities, the participants identify areas of developmental need and negotiate a training programme which can be tailored to the context in which staff are working.

The essential communication processes needed for a successful supervision relationship to arise cannot be left to chance. Thus, training for supervisors could usefully include training for doctoral students including guidelines which may de-mystify the process of producing a thesis, including: What is meant by originality? What should my expectations of feedback be? How often? How much? In what form? (Zuber-Skerritt & Ryan 1994).

However, the low response rate to Zuber-Skerritt and Ryan's study together with additional comments offered by students imply that supervisors and students prefer to describe their experiences in a more personal manner, and the application of any other method to identify training needs may not capture the intensely personal journey undertaken by a supervisor and student. Indeed, any doctoral supervision is frequently referred to as a 'private space' (see Manathunga, 2002) in which the development of an intense, individual relationship between tutor and protégé results in the student learning how to become an independent researcher by observing the supervisor. Whilst practitioner researchers at doctoral level may be assigned two supervisors in the research stage, in practice they may work mainly with one, which might be described as a continuation of the single tutor/apprentice model, and the intense nature of this relationship is maintained.

Implications of expanded higher education for supervision

Expansion of higher education is driving universities in new directions and to continue to supervise ever-growing numbers of students in conventional ways may fast become untenable (Clark, 1994), not least in finding enough time for supervisors to attend face-to-face meetings with their students. This applies equally well to the difficulties some higher education institutions are facing with professional doctorate supervision, since year on year there are ever-increasing numbers of professional doctorate students but a relatively small pool of suitably qualified and available academics to supervise them. Using computer-based communications and digital technology offers a rational and practical solution to some of the difficulties of finding enough supervisors to work face-to-face with large numbers of practitioner research students based away from the university.

These approaches generate more rather than fewer training needs for supervisors, to support supervisors' IT skills and prevent poor use of ICT having a negative impact on the quality of the student experience. Supervision offers thoroughly 'situated learning' in terms of place, but it does not necessarily follow that competence in one form of supervision (face-to-face interaction) can unproblematically be transferred to another such as electronic or 'distance' supervision. As more international students are registered on UK doctoral programmes, the need for advanced skills in IT and other forms of training in effective 'distance' supervision may become more pressing; this is not an area specifically reserved for professional doctorate supervisors since supervisors of international PhD students and other distance students face similar issues. It is likely that supervision at a distance will have both electronic and telecommunications components, and these developments will add potential to the repertoire of forms of interaction between doctoral researcher and supervisor, even though the working knowledge of each about the other's practices may be even less well understood.

These challenges are very exciting for doctoral pedagogues and designers of doctoral curricula, for it is clear that practices of supervision are changing. What is less clear is how beliefs and values about doctoral knowledge are conveyed in these new means of communication, and we would suggest that this is an area worthy of exploration.

Chapter 8

Impact of doctoral research and researcher identity

Publicity material for the practitioner research doctoral degrees is frequently couched in terms of the degree enabling, through research, participants to impact on their employing institutions. In this chapter this claim is examined. We consider 'impact' from the empirical perspective of our own studies. In our study there was no doubt that participants thought that undertaking practitioner research at doctoral level had an impact on their practice in the way people thought about their work. However, there was less evidence to suggest wider influence.

In exploring questions of impact, we turn once again to activity theory of Engeström (2001), and discuss how this theory relates to theories of situated learning (Lave, 1988) and community of practice (Lave & Wenger, 1991; Wenger, 1998) that are frequently adopted to justify the professional doctorate as being a degree that relates to practice. Engeström shows that for learning to happen in a setting, relations between the setting, i.e. its history, cultural milieu, ambition and the learners – who they are, why they are there, what they think they are learning – are not just critical, but frame learning of the individual. He argues that these relations also affect the setting itself, in ways that cannot be anticipated, because the learning in these conditions forms new knowledge, not predicted in advance. Thus we suggest that this forms a very individual scenario for students, in which the notion of impact itself is problematic. We consider impact in relation to practice, to the research process, on the institutions involved and how these combine in helping to shape researcher identity.

What is a research degree for?

For people working professionally the question arises as to the purpose of a research degree: what is it for, and what does acquiring one enable the person acquiring it to do? Several professions such as teaching, social work and health care have postgraduate qualifications integrated into a framework for professional development that continues the initial or pre-service preparation. It is becoming more and more expected, and in some countries it is mandatory, that the professional continues with professional development post-qualifying up to masters level. Sometimes this process of ongoing postgraduate development begins as a part of the initial qualification framework, as in the case of teacher preparation in North America. In this chapter we explore what might change for a professional person undertaking doctoral study.

But insider research can be understood in other ways too. There is a large contingent of people moving into higher education as lecturer-practitioners. These people are employed in order to teach or train new entrants to their professions in the public services: social work, education or health. As has been pointed out by, for example, Griffiths *et al.* (2010) and Murray (2008), for lecturer-practitioners to conduct research alongside their work as mainstream trainers of other professionals is by no means straightforward, and does not happens automatically without specific interventions such as undertaking a research degree, or being guided by a research mentor, or undertaking research collaboratively with more experienced researchers. People also enter higher education from other professional fields specifically in order to undertake research, being employed in the academy in such ways as research fellows on projects. For these people, insiderness means being part of the university environment, and undertaking a doctoral study is part of the cultural adaptation necessary to thrive in that environment. It is through conducting research that such individuals join the community of practice of researchers in higher education.

Impact and public service policy

Despite the difficulties in driving policy forward through research, evidence is beginning to inform social policy, and government departments are actively seeking research input. Nevertheless this is a complex process as research evidence is not the only factor in determining what to do, and there is the occasional very public spat with high-profile resignations when policy appears to fly in the face of the research evidence. Hillage *et al.*'s (1998) review of research in schools showed that, broadly, policy regarding schools is largely uninformed by research, for research tends to be small-scale, incapable of generating findings that are reliable and generalisable and insufficiently based on existing knowledge. Research is also, according to this review, damned for being inaccessible and researcher-driven. In fact, according to a study reported by Davies (2007), in the Treasury in the UK, where ministers and senior officials makers actually turn for advice and opinion is, in rank order: special advisers; experts; professional associations; think tanks/opinion-formers; lobbyists and pressure groups; the media; constituents, consumers and users; with academic research coming in last of all.

Thus it seems that professionals conducting practitioner research at doctoral level will probably not be expecting their findings to change policy at national or international levels in their professional sphere. Rather, we are searching for some more subtle indications of impact, such increased influence or personal effectiveness in practice, improved practice, job satisfaction perhaps, and personal and/or professional growth or development. Scott *et al.*'s study (2004) discusses the impact of a professional doctorate on 'professional performance'. Wellington and Sikes reject the notion of performance:

> This is not a term that we would use since our experience over 10 years is that, in many instances, 'performance' is the wrong word – it is more a case that the doctorate has had influence and impact (sometimes obliquely) on professional attitude, disposition and confidence rather than directly affecting 'performance'.
>
> (2006: 724)

The reasons that people give for starting a doctorate are not the same as their perceptions of it having completed it. In Chapter 2 we discussed how people come to a professional doctorate in preference to a traditional PhD. As well as being drawn to the idea of links with practice, and working in a cohort, these experienced professionals are lured by the idea of there being a 'taught' component. However, links between practice and taught elements are tenuous and require thought to make them work.

Universities' claims

From the point of view of the university, as Neumann (2005) argues, sustaining distinctions between types of doctorate may help to justify attracting new and different target audiences to the programmes. In her study, conducted across six high-profile universities in Australia, respondents who were academics, from their experience of working with doctoral students, regarded the PhD and professional doctorates as pretty much the same. However, respondents who were either administrators or doctoral students did not and, especially at the early stages of doctoral work, regarded the professional doctorate as second-rate. Neumann argues that comparisons between the two routes consistently highlight similarities between doctoral degrees, and suggests that the main differences actually are the target populations and selection criteria, for professional doctorates usually insist upon applicants having two to three years of professional experience as well as academic qualifications at masters level. Because in Australia fees are charged for professional doctorates but not for PhD study, new names for doctoral study enable universities to extend their reach and increase their income. In fact, the degrees seem to be interchangeable, and the study identified several individuals who moved between programmes.

So, as part of the preparation for this book, we looked at some university websites to see how practitioner research at doctoral level, most usually the professional doctorate, is presented, and how the traditional doctorate is presented at the same institutions. All the extracts included were found on the same day in February 2009. This snapshot survey of publicity material, of universities in the UK, Canada and Australasia, shows a surprising variety in the way that professional doctorates are promoted. This is even more surprising given that the PhD has a much more consistent, though significantly understated, profile in the same institutions. The PhD is described almost entirely in terms of undertaking research, with sometimes an indication of support provided for research students. For example, my (Pat's) own institution is typical: 'The aim of the MPhil/DPhil programme is to provide the support and resources necessary to complete a substantial piece of research which, in most cases, has an empirical component.' At the time of writing, we could not find any claims regarding possible future advantages of undertaking a research degree of this type, nor any claims of how a PhD might be relevant professionally or in other ways. This is in contrast with the EdD, where institutions appear to fall over themselves to point up the benefits of undertaking study of this kind.

Some professional doctorate publicity, for example, focuses on relevance to professional practice, such as this first extract, also taken from Pat's university: 'Work at doctoral level on issues that are of direct relevance to their own professional interests and institutional concerns.' Others, such as the two following, from England and Canada respectively, emphasise relations between generating new knowledge and practitioner learning, each making explicit the benefits of a research approach to developing professional knowledge:

> It provides health and social care professionals worldwide with lifelong learning in a manner that suits their professional and personal commitments.

> The program is grounded in the belief that it is important for participants to engage in scholarly discourse about understanding, critiquing and improving practice in educational settings.

These benefits are connected in this further UK example, through the idea of critical reflection on the part of the researcher: 'The degree is intended for experienced educational psychologists who would like to develop their professional expertise, carry out research relevant to their professional practice, and reflect critically on their work and their role.'

In some cases, grand claims (we think probably largely unfounded) are made for the professional advantage gained by someone completing a practitioner research degree:

- 'advanced learning which achieves major organizational change' (a UK university);
- 'Will enable candidates to develop sound policy in medicines management and to provide leadership in the profession through research' (an Australasian university);
- 'will enhance the careers of senior managers with educational responsibilities in any form of organisation' (another UK university).

Sometimes, different professional doctorates in the same institution focus differently, as in the case of a professional doctorate in health and social care at Linda's university, and the EdD at the same institution. The first emphasises that the researcher is likely to be open-minded and to resist certainty, whilst the second claims that the researcher will be able to 'resolve' problems in practice – almost the antithesis, apparently.

> Research-based study at doctoral level is expected to lead to the generation of original knowledge, and this implies a greater intolerance of closure and resolution of issues and controversies, and a correspondingly higher level of tolerance for complexity and uncertainty.

Contrasts with:

> This innovative EdD course is intended for experienced, practising education professionals. It supports their development as researching practitioners with a critical and interrogative approach to the resolution of problems in educational practice.

These extracts illustrate perfectly the nature of the tension we explore in this chapter. What is the impact of doctoral endeavour as a practitioner, and how does undertaking a doctoral degree at work affect the professional practice, and shape the identity of the practitioner researcher? What, if any, relations are there between researcher identity and professional practice, and how are these balanced and nuanced?

Impact in relation to practice

Neumann (2005) showed that rather than the outcomes of professional doctorate research making a difference to practice, the only link between academia and the practice setting was in the student's involvement and interest in the project. This tenuous link between research and practice is called further into question by student perceptions that the benefit of a professional doctorate will translate into career advancement. In Neumann's study this was negative in some cases and at best marginal in others. More recent work by Leonard (2009) suggests that neither are there career benefits for doctoral researchers completing traditional PhDs in the UK. Neumann argues that professional doctorates can be regarded as 'federal policy on the part of universities' (2005: 185), who seek to sustain artificial distinctions in order to recruit more students. We consider this from the empirical perspective of our own studies. In our earlier study (2008) of 13 participants (see Chapter 1 for details of the participants) on the professional doctoral programme, there was no doubt that participants thought that undertaking practitioner research at doctoral had an impact on the individual's practice in the way people thought about their work. However, there was less evidence to suggest wider influence. Brennan *et al.* (2002) have noted that doctoral students applying their ideas professionally tend to be quite senior, and as one person pointed out to us: 'there's a sort of assumption ... that you're going to come along and actually reflect on your practice and do something about it ... and of course that assumes you are a decision-maker at a fairly senior level' (Simon, a secondary school teacher). And in our study, the people who were able to claim some impact were indeed senior decision-makers, such as the headteacher who said:

> I'm a lot tougher with colleagues about what they write and how they write and the messages they give ... one of the things I think I'm encouraging colleagues to do more research, sharing a lot of information I've written for the doctorate with colleagues. So I do feel that out of it comes a responsibility to work with others.
>
> (Jonathan, a secondary headteacher quoted in Drake & Heath, 2008: 138)

We have extended our previous work through more conversations in the UK and in Australia with five people who have recently (within the last five years) completed their doctorates, and a further three who are on the doctoral programme (details of participants in Chapter 1).

Four of the completers are working in higher education as lecturers or researchers, and at the time of the conversation one was a deputy principal in a 4–14 campus school. Of the people who are not yet finished, one is a primary school principal, one a primary teacher and one a lecturer in higher education. The conversations took place over April–May 2009 and were conducted both face-to-face and by email. Our intention was to explore the question of impact explicitly, as this had arisen from the analysis of data collected in our earlier study and had become an organisational category. Respondents were invited to engage with the following questions:

1   Why did you do a doctorate?
2   How was it possible for you to do a doctorate?
3   Does it make a difference to nature of work now?
4   Does it make a difference in terms of job security?
5   Does it make a difference to the way you feel about your work?
6   Is there anyone who helps and encourages you?

The relationship of doctoral study to practice is discussed in the next sections of the chapter.

We are concerned that a focus on the professional doctorate per se may mask aspects of doing a doctorate as a practitioner, regardless of whether the doctorate was a professional doctorate or a traditional PhD. Earlier in this chapter we referred to the secondary headteacher who, having completed his doctorate, demanded more from the teachers in his school in terms of the way they wrote about practice. This is mirrored in the views of several of our respondents too, who, regardless of the name of their doctorate (EdD, PhD, DPhil), explained how their doctorates provided critical perspectives, not just on what had been researched, but on the way everything was viewed: teaching, employment, other research. As one said about her DPhil: 'it almost affects my approach to life, including the way I read newspaper articles, the discipline of doing a thesis stays with you' (Teresa, a university lecturer). One of our email correspondents wrote about the professional doctorate:

> I have a deeper understanding of why things work or don't work. That has been a source of almost joy – to be able to explain good practice that I observe through theory and to be able to articulate that. I think that was the problem before. I knew what was working from experience, but couldn't give the reasons why.
>
> (Anna, a school deputy principal)

Mary is a primary headteacher beginning the fourth year of her professional doctorate. Her research is as an insider, for she is working to raise the mathematics attainment in her inner-city primary school, a school with several problems associated with poverty and deprivation: under-attainment, a transient refugee and early immigrant population and, until recently, low staff morale. Mary has as part of her research so far visited other schools, and conducted an extensive literature review into learning and teaching mathematics. Her preferred and chosen approach to the next stage of her project is to establish an action learning set to explore in school mathematics teaching and learning in a focused and relevant way for her school. Mary believes that her doctoral study has impacted on her professional practice, in so far as she is no longer willing to accept criticism about the school from outside sources such as the local authority and the schools inspectorate without politely challenging the basis for these assertions. She feels much more confident as a leader and more able to support her staff, and more than that, provide broad and research-informed advice in response to their questions.

This perception that doctoral study enables practice to be understood more clearly pervades most of our conversations. This critical purchase on aspects of professional life enables the person to change, sometimes subtly, ways that they go about their work, and things that they do, in ways that without a doctorate may not have been possible. One person, a contract researcher on a large international project, had been appointed to the post before completing her (traditional) doctorate. We were told: 'I feel more confident about being critical and communicating with others and this is implicit and shared with other team members. We create a standard. I have taken on more of this since I completed my doctorate' (Jenny, a research fellow). Another university teacher (Christine) believes that her traditional doctorate made a significant difference 'as it sets up a level of expectation in research, on me and on others, through reviewing: conference papers and research bids'.

Practitioners reflect on the impact of doing their doctorates in different ways. Some refer to ways of working having improved, for example, Jonathan: 'I think my own practice has probably, yes it has, it's changed in terms of, I've got a very disciplined approach to work and document writing and various things to do with reporting and accountability.' This headteacher also changed jobs during the time of his doctoral studies, and reflects that this combination of moving professionally and researching teachers helped professionally when coming to terms with new work environments:

Having worked in one school that had failed and then improved, working across the county and then going north..., that information that I was drawing out of what teachers were saying, was helping me work in new settings, probably better. So I was well aware that it was directly impacting on my own work.

In terms of employment, having completed a doctorate seems, from our respondents, not necessarily to offer much in the way of immediate professional advantage. For those working in higher education, completing a doctorate as an insider signals that a transitional stage into academic life has been completed. This puts the person at the bottom of a new professional ladder, rather than being at the top of a previous one. Of our respondents, some relinquished professional careers in order to become a graduate student; all were working part-time, and only one had a permanent contract. Promotion prospects were a long way off for people whose main preoccupation was to secure a permanent job. Our informants told us that life as a member of a project team, or with a teaching contract, left little time for further research or writing up for publication. Ironically, one person, Christine, explained that her fortunate and independent financial security enabled her to pick and choose the work she became involved with, and that she was seriously considering leaving the university altogether in order to work on publishing from the thesis. Work by Leonard supports this, showing that of three groups of people undertaking traditional doctorates, one group, the research fellows on projects, were the most disaffected group. In the Neumann study, very few students on any of the doctoral programmes had enrolled in order to get ahead in their careers.

> The tenuous link between research and practice is called further into question by student perceptions that the benefits of a professional doctorate for career advancement is negative in some cases and at best marginal in others. This perception is in sharp contrast to the aims printed in faculty recruiting brochures.
>
> (2005: 185)

We note that in England, despite concerns on the part of universities to recruit staff that already have a doctorate as expressed in the numerous job descriptions and advertisements, lecturer-practitioners are frequently appointed, particularly into teacher education and social work preparation, without doctoral credentials. This is mirrored by one of our Australian respondents, a lecturer in higher education who wrote:

> Originally, I thought doing a doctorate was very important in terms of job security and this was made very clear to me while I was working as a sessional member of staff and then while I was on a fixed term contract. But I secured a permanent position in November 2008 and there were no specific requirements in the contract that the doctorate would be completed.
>
> (Margaret, a university lecturer)

Our respondents who had completed professional doctorates were all in full-time work, and were senior too: two school principals and a deputy principal of a school campus for 4–14-year-olds. We've drawn upon Jonathan's experience already. He moved jobs twice whilst completing the doctorate, especially choosing to move away from the school where data had been collected so as to write up without being compromised by the need to sustain collegial relations in the school whilst being very critical of it. Anna noted wryly that, whilst doing her doctorate had made her restless and hopeful of a bigger challenge from a post with more scope, applying for posts was not proving successful.[1] She told us: 'I have been short listed on every occasion. One principal phoned quite apologetically to say that I was by far the best candidate, but they felt the doctorate would be intimidating to their staff.' So any impact of completing doctoral work on practice is to start with in terms of an enhanced ability to discern, understand and be critical about professional life. We would question the ways in which having a doctorate raises the career profile of the individual, particularly those working in higher education, and suggest that higher education in particular may operate in a duplicitous manner. People without doctorates are appointed, particularly to lecturer-practitioner posts, but told that they need complete a thesis otherwise promotion will be limited; and people with doctorates who undertake these studies whilst working inside higher education on short-term research contracts find that without publications, successfully obtaining research grants and teaching experience, they are no more likely to be appointed to permanent positions than they were originally. Our sample is very small, but two of the school teachers completing, Jonathan and Anna, have moved out of the school section into advisory and development positions in education. The trajectory of teachers completing practitioner doctorates would be of interest in a future research, given the concerns expressed by Hargreaves (1999, 2007) and discussed earlier in this volume that educational research is not undertaken by practising practitioners.

Shaping researcher identity

Scott *et al.* (2004) suggest that doing a professional doctorate means different things to different people, according to the stage the person is at in their career; on the identity that the person wishes to enact; upon the relationships, beliefs and values that are important in their lives; and upon their previous biography. Wellington and Sikes illustrate this, suggesting that previous critical incidents – and they give the example of failing the eleven-plus examination – may have a direct bearing on the motivation of the person to undertake doctoral study, for instance as a means of overcoming previous perceived failure. This suggests that doing the doctorate affirms a positive sense of identity. For many it was a combination of reasons:

> I'd reached a point in my life where I needed something more. My job at that time did not offer many challenges and I felt I was 'coasting'.... Another factor, looking back, was that I felt dissatisfied in other areas of my life also – but not enough to do anything about them. So, I decided to do something that was just for me: it would boost my confidence ... it might also help me get a bit more noticed by others within my current HEI [higher education institution] ... and, finally and probably most importantly, I wanted to get back into learning for its own sake myself.
>
> (2006: 728)

Crossouard and Pryor (2008) argue that, as the process of undertaking doctoral study necessarily involves a change of identity – 'becoming a researcher' – this process of identity-formation is a part of the process of learning. As we have proposed in Chapters 6 and 7, learning is not about acquisition of new knowledge per se. For a practitioner coming to research, starting with a distinction between 'practitioner' and 'researcher' may provide a useful contrast, a beginning point for considering different ways of developing a perspective on a researchable situation. As has been argued consistently throughout this book, this distinction is not sustainable for most doctoral work, for becoming a researcher almost always involves integration between academic and professional practice through a process of reflexive engagement, and this reflexivity lasts beyond the end of the project.

However, in marked contrast, George, another headteacher of a primary school, considered the impact of the insider research (for an EdD) to be primarily during the research process. Having enrolled on the degree, he explicitly looked for a project to undertake for doctoral study, and found that developing ICT networks and support fitted the bill. George talked enthusiastically about conducting the research and its relevance to the school:

> Once the doctoral thesis began, even before, I wanted the focus of the study to benefit the school that I work at. So it had to be in an area where primary schools and primary practitioners were struggling and for me it was just so obvious ... that was the first thing that I felt with the EdD. If you were going to get through it you had to be passionate about an area that really affected you in your workplace.

Once completed though, George, at the time of the interview less than one year after completion, talked about his EdD as in the past, over and done with: 'My interest now is almost, you've done it and that's it.' He couldn't remember, when asked the title of the thesis, what it was called: 'It was a long title. Do you want it now? I need to just look at my computer.' For this person, undertaking the doctorate was a means to an end, and, once the end was reached, serving no further purpose.

Clearly, doing the doctorate means different things to different people.

We have shown in this chapter that insiderness in terms of being or becoming a researcher through doctoral study means different things. To some insider researchers, like those on professional doctorates who work in a practice setting such as schools or colleges, insider research is likely to mean researching one's own workplace. Others, employed as lecturer-practitioners, training teachers or social workers or health professionals, are insiders in the sense of being employed by a higher education institution, but outsiders in their relationship to their previous professional base. Yet another group consists of researchers on projects, also employed by universities, who undertake doctoral study alongside their project. These employees in higher education apparently outnumber other doctoral students in education (Leonard, 2009).

Engaging with doctoral study as an insider can mean undertaking either a traditional or a professional doctorate. We are left wondering at the end of this chapter about the hyperbole regarding doctoral study, particularly the professional doctorate, for which great claims are made. Can the professional doctorate and the insider research undertaken during it be viewed merely and cynically as a recruitment drive on the part of universities seeking to exploit a target group of reasonably wealthy mid-career professionals looking to channel their enquiring minds and tendency towards overwork? And for those mid-career professionals who move into higher education as professional educators, is the doctorate a distraction that inhibits career development?

We conclude by suggesting that, considered in terms of the impact of completing a doctoral degree on the identity of the person, both traditional doctorates and professional doctorates generate feelings of confidence, security and enhanced critical understanding. For professionals this is expressed in terms of deeper understanding of professional practices and processes, and the ability to consider centralised intervention from an informed perspective. For people employed within the university this manifests in the form of enhanced criticality regarding documentation – articles, proposals and other students' work – and also in terms of perceiving inequities in the organisation of the institutions that explicitly encourage the labour of doctoral study whilst refusing to reward it in material ways. Neither degree provides any immediate career prospects, certainly not in the short term, either within higher education or within the professional field. As participants in communities of practice bring new experiences to the practices, practice gradually and over time changes. So whilst the impact of an individual's contribution may not be apparent, the fact of an increased (or decreased) research focus will eventually change the way that practice is thought about.

Everyone seems to be delighted at having been successful, and as one person said:

> Actually the thing about a doctorate for me that is interesting is the way that other people are so pleased for you and see it as important rather than any difference it makes to the way I see myself or professionally.
>
> (Ella, a university lecturer)

Chapter 9

Integrating academic and professional knowledge

Writing the thesis

Completing doctoral research involves writing. Whilst evidence of working at doctoral level in practices such as music or art or media or creative writing may involve presenting original contributions to the genre, such as composition, artworks, film or creative writing, it is also the case that these forms are accompanied by a written exegesis or analytical commentary. For practitioners in professional fields such as education, social work and health, completing doctoral work means submitting a significant thesis that sets out the case for an original contribution to knowledge. Successfully defending a written thesis, or for practitioners in the creative arts defending an exegesis, in an oral examination is the usual way that the candidate convinces the examiners that the work is deserving of the doctoral degree. Doctoral researchers all face a huge challenge in putting together a credible thesis, for it is through the thesis that their research stands or falls. This challenge has particular significance for researchers investigating the inside of professional settings. As has been discussed throughout this book so far, insiders are conducting their projects adroitly managing tensions between their workplace, the awarding university and their own transformative project in achieving a doctorate.

There are two immediate dimensions to this challenge. First, the thesis is a text, an object, indeed a measurable output, that stands for all the work that has gone into it. In Chapter 4 we discussed text as representation and how the validity of the project is discerned through the extent to which the text is recognised by others in the field. We have suggested throughout that the apparent simplicity of practitioner research activity is actually very complex and requires fluidity on the part of the researcher. This fluidity now extends to the performance of text-making, of representation of the work in relation to researcher position, because it is through the text that the new knowledge is presented. As we have argued, this new knowledge arises from integrating professional learning with personal transformation as the candidate succeeds in the practices of higher education. Second, and related to the above, there is a challenge in so far as the author must use language developed within conventional forms of knowledge-making to take a position and to present knowledge that may at first sight appear at odds with conventional forms. However, notions of distinctly different doctoral awards underpinned by a different language, different forms of knowledge and so on, as we have argued, no longer really convince.

We have suggested throughout this book that whilst practitioner research may appear deceptively simple, it is actually very complex because of the difficulty of establishing a position with respect to insider/outsiderness that is consistent with expectations of critical purchase on the process of research. This fluidity of position means that the way the work is represented in print, i.e. the thesis or in other published material, must include some exploration on the part of the author as to how the text comes into being. This challenge first arose in postmodern discourse and plays out in practical and real ways for doctoral practitioner researchers. The challenge of postmodernism (discussed with respect to knowledge construction in Chapter 4) continues to be manifest in the construction of the object that conveys this new knowledge.

This chapter is not a 'how to write a thesis' chapter, for there are plenty of these published already. Kamler and Thompson show how by not addressing the complexity of doctoral writing as being work on text/identity, this self-help genre of 'how to' feeds on the anxiety of doctoral researchers through assertive 'transmission pedagogies that normalize the power-saturated relations of protégé and master' (2008: 504). Kamler and Thompson point to the desirability of 'alternate pedagogical approaches that position doctoral researchers as colleagues engaged in a shared, unequal, and changing practice' (2008: 504). We argue also that originality cannot be attained though generalised instructional self-help. This is because new understandings of the relationship between practical and theoretical knowledge have moved away from the dual model developed by Gibbons *et al.* (1994) of Mode One propositional and Mode Two experiential knowledge. We have also moved away from the more complex suggestions of an additional two modes of knowledge, Mode Three (encompassing deliberation and action) and Mode Four (concerned with the development of the individual through critical reflection) from Scott (1995), discussed previously in Chapter 7.

The study, which may be ongoing in practice beyond the completion of the doctorate, and the resulting written thesis exemplify an endeavour of professional reflexion-in-action. In grappling with inherent challenges of research methodology arising out of overt personal involvement, the study also becomes a project in representation, in authenticity, in authorial and researcher voice. Acknowledging these dimensions requires the author of the thesis to think carefully about the genre of their writing, of the extent to which they place themselves in the text, their authorial responsibilities as storyteller of other inform-ants. The thesis becomes a representation of their own thoughts, even though these may be explicitly informed by the stated perspectives of others.

Creating new knowledge

Rather than continue to categorise new forms of knowledge in an increasingly lengthy list, in this chapter we propose a more radical stance. We have argued throughout this book that practitioner research-ers engage with new knowledge at all stages of the project, from concep-tualisation through methodology, methods and empirical work to the thesis. We suggest that new knowledge derives from all these dimensions of the study, informs all aspects under consideration at each stage, and is both directly connected to undertaking the project at all in a practice setting and unique to each researcher and their research. This absence of replicability needs to be explained in the thesis, and as we argued in Chapter 4 leads to a unique, relativist 'grounded methodology' that also needs to be explained.

We continue to assert that new knowledge is necessarily unique, and that this uniqueness arises out of any combination of several or indeed all of the following: research questions and findings; grounded meth-odological position; situated ethical position; changed perceptions of work through developing identity as a researcher. In this chapter we discuss what this may mean for practitioner doctoral researchers, what shapes the thesis text to convince that new knowledge is indeed repre-sented within its pages and how participating in these practices relates to identity work.

The relationship between concepts, ideas and theories and the relev-ance and application of these in professional settings is a central concept (see, for example, Eraut, 2004b) in bridging the theory–professional knowledge gap. In university departments of professional education such as education, social work and health, the discourse of researching one's own practice is central to professional and academic work with postgraduate researchers. These 'students' are, most fre-quently, practising professionals such as teachers or social workers looking for means of investigating their practice. Faculty research in education departments in universities is in continual tension with teaching. High stakes and high status, education research is further riven with debate as to the relative merits of different approaches to it. For example, the benefits or otherwise of randomised controlled trials or of systematic reviewing (e.g. McClure, 2003; Oakley *et al.*, 2003) are hotly discussed. These binaries are significant in that attention is focused on research findings, how these are established, whether they can be applied, and how these relate to the means of producing them. In other words, focus on these polarised ways on findings is also a focus on methodological and textual issues, and raises awareness of problems inherent in bringing such work to readers at all (e.g. Dunne *et al.*, 2005). These discussions rage in public and in print (Sebba, 2007; Torrance & Sebba, 2007).

In professional settings, 'research' is becoming a very seductive word, conveying as it does the use of considered and thoughtful intelligence to analysing problems and seeking a means of moving forwards in addressing them. Increasingly, as well as through alignment with university departments, practitioners are encouraged to undertake research in a variety of other ways. For example, the National College of School Leadership (NCSL) offers grants for practitioners in schools to develop specific aspects of school leadership. Project reports and case studies are published on the NCSL website (www.ncsl.org.uk), with summary guidance from these findings set out for school leaders interested in developing practice in their own establishments. In this way development and research undertaken by grant holders is recognised as making a contribution to knowledge about school leadership, and is exposed to a wider audience. However, as these studies are not published in recognised academic outlets, these 'findings' would not be picked up either through systematic reviewing or through discussion of the substantive methodologies, and so are not considered part of the canon of academic output, despite their presentation being designed explicitly to have a direct impact on practice.

So there is a wide continuum of educational research, and practitioner researchers at doctoral level are located between the extremes. Drawn to engage with methodological issues, practitioner doctoral researchers have access to research discourse in academia and are motivated to find a means of addressing problems in day-to-day work. It is ironic that whilst research is in tension with teaching for faculty in university departments of education, the professional doctorate degree requires the candidate to manage precisely this tension between research and practice in the micro-context of problem-solving at work. In the UK, studies are likely to be small-scale, with audience limited to the supervisor and examiners and, if we include the chair of the viva, one more person. In North America, Europe and Australasia the thesis defence may be open also to an invited audience. Subsequent publication of articles potentially broadens the extent of the audience, but it seems safe to say that most insider doctoral researchers do not conduct their studies primarily motivated by the idea that the results will appear in public. Nevertheless, writing and orally defending the thesis is extremely high stakes, for as Maher *et al.* (2008) point out, it is through this successful writing that doctoral candidates 'become peer', i.e. are recognised as having attained mastery over academic practices.

What is more, just as doctoral supervisors vary in attitude to ways of knowing, so too are assessors of the thesis are likely to read it differently according to their own predilections and interests. For instance, some may be more interested in practice-related issues such as how useful it is, with others more concerned with the robustness of the approach. Hargreaves (2007) has argued that good research should be plausible, relevant to legitimate public concerns and high-quality, and that, unfortunately, often education research is none of these. Certainly, the examination of the thesis is going to focus on the credibility of the account. As Scott *et al.* (2004) explain, this has meant various checks, according to the paradigm in which the study is presented; classically this would mean checking representativeness, internal validity, external validity and objectivity. Grounded theory (Lincoln & Guba, 1985) requires credibility, transferability, dependability, confirmability, that is, that the analysis is grounded in the data and that inferences based on the data are logical and useful. Later (1989), Guba and Lincoln ask that research also be catalytic and empowering (research as emancipation discourse is explained in Chapter 4). For practitioner research yet more considerations may be at play as well. For example, as Taylor (2003) suggests, additional criteria may arise from consideration of audience. The work may be judged on its accessibility and appropriateness for the community of practice to which the knowledge is related.

There is an important idea that comes from the work of Bakhtin (1981) that can help provide a purchase on the challenges posed above. The idea is heteroglossia. Bakhtin uses the term 'utterance' to convey something that is said or written, be this as small a unit as a word, or as large a unit as a whole book. Heteroglossia proposes an interaction between 'utterance' text as part of linguistic system, and utterance as having specific and unique contextual power, which adds or subtracts meaning from independent manifestation of system of text. This means that whilst there are many words and combinations of words in each and every linguistic system and in each and every language, what these 'utterances' actually mean are also entirely connected to the context in which they are spoken or written. Bakhtin suggests that language is 'saturated' with social meanings, and so:

> All words have the 'taste' of a profession, a genre, a generation, an age group, the day and hour. Each word tastes of the context and contexts in which it has lived its socially charged life; all words and forms are populated by intentions.
>
> (1981: 293)

This means that, for the researcher constructing the thesis text, audience is extremely important, for readers will recognise the substantive ideas through the forms of language by which they are expressed.

Becoming author

Following the deconstruction movement associated with Derrida (1982; Derrida & Bass, 2001) and Barthes (1970), postmodernists (e.g. Schostak, 2000; MacLure, 2003) develop the reflexivity initiated by, for example, Burgess (1985) and others. Derrida has shown us the web of 'structure, sign and play' of social relations, how textual differences are not always apparent in the social relations themselves, and vice versa. Any text purporting to describe, report on or analyse events in the world inevitably does so only as an interpretation in recognition that the text stands as a mediator between the author (who is indescribable) and the 'Other', i.e. outside the author, also indescribable. There is nothing outside the text, no extra 'truth' that the text approximates to. Partiality in an account is therefore inevitable, given that invariably there are multiple perspectives on any situation or event. MacLure (2003) argues that the thing itself, in its absence, cannot be witness to a representative validity. So for research to have any meaning it is not a matter of looking harder or more closely, but of seeing what frames our seeing, of exploring the spaces we construct, of looking critically at what the research chooses to make visible.

Erben argues that stories of self are an important means of understanding 'complex and unclear social situations' (2002: 416). Particularly in the field of life history, research writers such as West and Alexopoulou (1993), and Stuart (1993), make explicit the part that the private writings, thoughts and theories of the researcher play in shaping the research process. Stuart (1993) points to the impossibility of excluding herself and her opinions when interviewing. She relates this to a feminist perspective developed in Stanley's work on auto/biography (see, for example, 1993), in which the self or identity is posited as a major contributing factor on both the development of the research question and the research itself. About herself and her work, Stanley wrote on her website:

> the analytic term 'auto/biography' stands for an approach which challenges the supposed binaries of self and other, fact and fiction, past and present, reality and representation, autobiography and biography; and although by no means coterminous with feminism, nonetheless the project of auto/biography has much in common with that of feminism/Women's Studies.
>
> (Stanley, 1999)

Stuart builds on Stanley's concept of self, as constructed by opposites including those structured by gender, social, class, age, race, etc. to show how this is crucial in building relationships with people contributing to the research, and that these relationships are two-way.

Writing a practitioner research project must bring together elements of performance, motivation, power, knowledge, mutual understanding and self-understanding. The text structures the researcher's subjectivity, is active, dynamic, searching for justification, knowledge and power over ideas, and must convince readers, who, if this is a doctoral thesis, will include one or two assessors, structured by the university as very powerful. Schostak (2000) explains that in using language one constructs a text outside oneself that allows us to explore each others' worlds. Recognising that meaning cannot ever be public or unambiguous, Schostak argues that if one brings something to people's attention, for a time that 'phenomenon' cannot be taken for granted. The best an author can do is to make explicit these tensions, and negotiate a process for conducting and writing that permits her to voice her own story, recognising as Rosen (1998) pointed out that, in text, there is an irony in the use of the word 'voice'. Dunne *et al.* (2005) discuss research and identity in a chapter 'The selfish text', and that is exactly what is needed – a methodological means of explicit selfishness. For it is not the respondents' version of reality that practitioner researchers are seeking to present, but their own, even though these personal interpretations may often be based on respondents' expressed perspectives.

Exploring the position of the author as integral to the research project brings several considerations together. Tierney points out that the omniscience of this voice nonetheless takes different forms:

> Although all authors must deal with issues such as the length of a text or the choice of data to include or exclude, what goes unquestioned is the manner in which the author presents him or herself in the text, the relationship one develops <u>in the text</u> with those involved in the study, and the temporal sequence in which the data gets presented.
>
> (1997: 24)

Tierney also points to the use of tense and how using present tense in an account invites the reader to go along with the author in revealing the tale, usually apparently realist, even though everyone knows that in some senses the author already knows the end. Creamer (2006) draws attention to how conventional social science texts, despite engaging with ideas of participant constructivism, generally take a 'single-authored' position in the text, regardless of whether the writing is co-authored or not. If it is single-authored, she points out the use of 'we' as a means of establishing authorial authority. She argues that authors use scripts or headings or conversations in writing, and points to a dilemma between telling a story to get the story told, and postmodern reflexivity that encourages polyvocality, but is hard to read. Like Lather and Smithies (1997), whose stance alongside women with HIV/AIDS is visible through a literal division of text on the page, Creamer claims that 'Polyvocalism that is undertaken as more than a token way to advance an argument challenges the assumption that no matter how many authors, a single person must be "in charge" of the text.' Confessional or romantic tales often follow later from a modernist or realistic account provided at the time of the project, in what Lincoln (1997) calls postmodern 'saturated self' accounts. The realistic account arises from the author's choice of an identity with which to write, with criteria for choice including consideration of audience and/or stakeholders, purpose of the text, potential for creating multiple texts, or the climate of policy. The confessional tale then allows the author to develop a reflexive and self-critical account of story previously presented as clean and unproblematic. However, whilst the confessional tale may be a route to reflexivity, in itself it is no guarantee that the uniquely personal story is robust enough to meet the demands for originality.

Ivanic (1998), in a project with mature undergraduate students, explored the development of academic writing with students as co-researchers. Through the project she identified three personae evident in the undergraduates' writing: personal self, which has an autobiographical flavour; discoursal self which is specifically located in the discourse of the discipline; and the authoritative persona which reflects a critical engagement with the discipline, and which in academic discourse is highly prized. Developing undergraduate writers largely experiment with personal voice and discipline-specific discourses, in contrast to experienced academic writers whose published work is set in authoritative discourse. Ivanic suggests that students are positioned by their tutors through their writing and that this positioning is so important that students, rather than simply trying to learn how to reproduce academic writing, 'should explore the way that different discourses position them, and discuss the personal and political consequences of participating in them' (1998: 340). She observes that writing in an authoritative manner is rarely taught, but the essays that were awarded the best marks exhibit it.

Bakhtin writes about the authoritative word thus:

> it binds us, quite independent of any power it might have to persuade us internally; we encounter it with its authority already fused

to it. … It is a prior discourse … it demands our unconditional allegiance … permits no play with the context framing it.

(1981: 342–343)

We learn to work in the authoritative discourse through a dialogic process of wresting meaning out of others' authoritative words that we have acknowledged and assimilated over time.

Writing reflexivity

I have written elsewhere (Drake, 2010) that exposing the clumsiness of research is a risky business, and some writers (for example, Paechter, 1996; Walford, 1998) would advise against it. Walford as an experienced doctoral examiner asserts that it is tedious to read 'the halting descriptions of inexperienced researchers' poor research' (1998: 4). Paechter argues that in the drive for methodological rigour in qualitative research, opening up research diaries and so on exposes the least powerful (whom she categorises as school teachers undertaking action research and PhD candidates) to scrutiny by the establishment, often to the individual disadvantage of the researcher, even if greater collective rigour is achieved for qualitative research methodology as a whole. She likens the process to the Judaeo-Christian tradition of confession of sins, and through this analogy implicitly questions Ball's (1990) advice to accompany research accounts with other self-revealing documentation, on the grounds that power relations are too strongly loaded against the doctoral candidate. Whichever way the candidate looks at these views, whilst of course hoping for a sympathetic examiner, they may be forgiven for adopting a lower-risk strategy.

Nevertheless, the insider researcher must consider themselves to be an integral element in the research process, and must think about how creating their research story – the choice of questions, the methodological approach, the methods and the analysis of the data – is connected to who they are, their previous experience, professional knowledge and desire to bring this into the academy via doctoral study. Hunt and Sampson define reflexivity

as the cognitive ability[1] to move fluidly back and forth between an inside and an outside perspective on oneself, giving oneself up to the experience of 'self as other' whilst also retaining a grounding in one's familiar sense of self.

(2006: 4)

Van Heugten states that the positivist concern with objectivity and detachment have predominated until relatively recently, whereas it is now more widely accepted that these ideals are impossible and perhaps undesirable in human research (2004: 207). In her reflexive accounts, she used a 'stream of consciousness' writing, interviewed herself in depth on tape and spoke to others about her experiences such as her supervisor and critical friends. These techniques were designed to create distance where it was possible and to begin to deconstruct the familiar world in which she worked.

Using one's diary as a research resource is a natural tool for reflexivity. Miller did her doctoral fieldwork in the mid-1970s, but didn't write up until rather later, to complete in 1989. By then she had doubts about the validity of her original project, and felt that 'to continue or repeat a research process when I was so uncertain about its value would be at best an empty ritual and at worst a fraudulent exercise' (1993: 88). She felt uneasy about the theoretical and methodological bases of her original project, but came to realise that there were other reasons for her reluctance and she writes about this in the preamble to her thesis, which she quotes:

> I recognized that my frequent desire to jettison the files of newspaper cuttings had been prompted by a mixture of confused and painful feelings. These were associated with the period as a research student, during which I left my husband, in the midst of a tangle of emotional and domestic turmoil. ... It was easier in the relative calm of 1983 to look back and react in an intellectual rather than emotional frame, but the events stamped into the fabric of my interview notes and coding sheets had for several years given me nightmares, quite literally.
>
> (1993: 10–11)

Part of my own (Pat's) doctorate involved re-visiting an uncompleted research study undertaken a few years previously. When writing this work up I re-read the analysis I had done of some interviews, and I also re-read my diary. The differences between these two sets of accounts was startling, and I write:

> The diary was a useful memory jogger, but more than that, by contrasting what was written in it with the stories constructed for the public domain from the interview accounts, it was possible to see the choices that might have been made, the selection and editing of material, and the partial 'truths' that eventually become public.
>
> (Drake, 2010: 97)

Writing a thesis is not simply a technical issue, for as we have shown, writing one's project is partial, according to one's degree of insiderness and position. Doctoral writing is situated in the professional setting and at the same time is constructed within the practice of academic writing that is culturally specific to doctoral work in Western countries. Very importantly, writing transforms the writer, for writing is a means of working out what one thinks. Working out what one thinks and expressing one's ideas in public can be an inestimably emotional and sometimes painful experience.

Writing this book has been no exception.

Good luck readers, and do keep going!

Notes

2 Professional doctorates: equal but different?

1 According to the QAA (2008) *Framework for higher education qualifications in England, Wales and Northern Ireland*.

Doctoral degrees are awarded for the creation and interpretation, construction and/or exposition of knowledge which extends the forefront of a discipline, usually through original research.

Holders of doctoral degrees will be able to conceptualise, design and implement projects for the generation of significant new knowledge and/or understanding. Holders of doctoral degrees will have the qualities needed for employment that require both the ability to make informed judgements on complex issues in specialist fields and an innovative approach to tackling and solving problems.

4 Approaching grounded methodology

1 Ian McEwan in his novel *Saturday* has the main character Henry Perowne reflect on Schrödinger's cat, concluding that the only thing that happens is that the opening of the box signals the disappearance of one's own ignorance.

8 Impact of doctoral research and researcher identity

1 Actually, since completing the EdD in 2010 this informant has gone on to a promotion.

9 Integrating academic and professional knowledge: writing the thesis

1 The term 'cognitive' here embraces conscious and unconscious mental processes (Lakoff & Johnson, 1980).

References

Adelman, C., Kemmis, S. & Jenkins, D. (1976) Rethinking case study: notes from the second Cambridge conference. *Cambridge Journal of Education*, 6 (3), 139–150.

Argyris, C. & Schön, D. (1978) *Organisational learning: a theory of action perspective*. London: Wiley.

Aristotle (350 BCE) *Nicomachean ethics*, trans. W.D. Ross. The Internet Classics archive, online: http://classics.mit.edu/Aristotle/nicomachaen.1.i.html. Accessed 13 May 2010.

Bakhtin, M.M. (1981) Discourse in the novel, trans. C. Emerson & M. Holquist. In M. Holquist (ed.), *The dialogic imagination*. Austin: University of Texas Press.

Ball, S.J. (1990) Self doubt and soft data: social and technical trajectories in ethnographic fieldwork. *Qualitative Studies in Education*, 3 (2), 157–171.

Barnett, R. (1990) *The idea of higher education*. Buckingham: Society for Research in Higher Education and Open University Press.

—— (1997) *Higher education: a critical business*. Buckingham: Society for Research in Higher Education and Open University Press.

—— (2000) *Realizing the university in an age of supercomplexity*. Buckingham: Society for Research in Higher Education and Open University Press.

Barthes, R. (1970) *Mythologies*. Paris: Seuil.

Becher, T. & Trowler, P.R. (2001) *Academic tribes and territories: intellectual enquiry and the culture of disciplines*, 2nd edn. Buckingham: Society for Research into Higher Education and Open University Press.

BERA (British Educational Research Association) (2004) Revised ethical guidelines for educational research. www.bera.ac.uk/files/2008/09/ethical.pdf.

Bernstein, B.B. (1999) Vertical and horizontal discourse: an essay. *British Journal of Sociology of Education*, 20 (2), 157–173.

—— (1996) *Pedagogy, symbolic control and identity: theory, research and critique*. London: Taylor & Francis.

Blaxter, L., Hughes, C. & Tight, M. (2001) *How to research*, 3rd edn. Buckingham: Open University Press.

Boud, D. & Lee, A. (eds) (2009) *Changing practices of doctoral education*. London: Taylor & Francis.

Boud, D. & Walker, D. (1990) *Reflection: turning experience into learning*. London: Kogan Page.

Bourdieu, P. (1988) *Homo academicus*. Cambridge: Polity Press.

—— (1997) *Outline of a theory of practice*. Cambridge: Cambridge University Press.

—— (2000) *Distinction: a social critique of the judgement of taste*. London: Routledge.

Bourner, T., Bowden, R. & Laing, S. (1999) A national profile of research degree awards: innovation, clarity and coherence. *Higher Education Quarterly*, 53 (3), 264–280.

—— (2001) Professional doctorates in England. *Studies in Higher Education*, 26 (1), 65–83.

—— (2002) Professional doctorates in the UK and Australia: not a world of difference. *Higher Education Review*, 35 (1), 76–87.

Brackenridge, C.H. (2001) *Spoilsports: understanding and preventing sexual exploitation in sport*. London: Routledge.

Bradford, S. (2007) The 'good youth leader': constructions of professionalism in English youth work, 1939–45. *Ethics and Social Welfare*, 1 (3), 293–309.

Bragg, M. (2008) *In our time*. BBC Radio 4, first broadcast 9.30 a.m., Thursday 18 December 2008.

Brennan, M. (1995) Education doctorates: reconstructing professional partnerships around research? *Australian Universities Review*, 38 (2), 20–22.

—— (1998) Struggles over the definition and practice of the educational doctorate in Australia. *Australian Educational Researcher*, 25 (1), 71–90.

Brennan, M., Kenway, J., Thomson, P. & Zipin, L. (2002) Uneasy alliances: university, workplace, industry and profession in the education doctorate. *The Australian Educational Researcher*, 29 (3), 63–84.

Brew, A. (2001) Conceptions of research: a phenomenographical study. *Studies in Higher Education*, 26 (3), 271–285.

Burgess, R.G. (1984) *The research process in educational settings: ten case studies*. Lewes: Falmer Press.

—— (1985) *Strategies of educational research*. Lewes: Falmer Press.

Campbell, A. & Groundwater-Smith, S. (eds) (2007) *An ethical approach to practitioner research*. London and New York: Routledge.

Carr, W. & Kemmis, S. (1986) *Becoming critical: education, knowledge and action research*. London: Falmer Press.

Chalmers, A.F. (1982) *What is this thing called Science?* 2nd edn. St Lucia, Queensland: University of Queensland Press.

Chandler-Grevatt, A., Clayton, S., Creaton, J., Crossland, J., Lefevre, M. & Robertson, S. (2008) *Unpicking the threads: Facebook, peer learning and the professional doctorate*. Paper presented at the Society for Research in Higher Education Postgraduate and Newer Researchers Conference, Liverpool.

Clark, B.R. (1994) The research–teaching nexus in modern systems of higher education. *Higher Education Policy*, 7 (1), 11–17.

Claxton, G.L. (1998, May) Knowing without knowing why. *The Psychologist*, May 1998, 217–220.

Coghlan, D. & Holian, R. (2007) Editorial: insider action research. *Action Research*, 5 (1), 5–10.

Creamer, E.G. (2006) Experimenting with voice and reflexivity in social science texts. In C. Conrad & R.C. Serlin (eds), *Sage handbook for research in education*. Thousand Oaks, CA: Sage, 529–542.

Crossouard, B. (2008) Developing alternative models of doctoral supervision with online formative assessment. *Studies in Continuing Education*, 30 (1), 51–67.

Crossouard, B. & Pryor, J. (2008) Becoming researchers: a sociocultural perspective on assessment, learning and the construction of identity in a professional doctorate. *Pedagogy, Culture & Society*, 16 (3), 221–237.

David, M. (2002) *Feminist contributions for doctoral education in Britain: feminist knowledge in the new knowledge economy*. Paper presented at the Fourth Biennial Conference on Professional Doctorates: Research Training for the Knowledge Economy, University of Queensland, Brisbane.

Davidson, A.I. (1994) Ethics as ascetics: Foucault, the history of ethics and ancient thought. In G. Gutting (ed.), *The Cambridge companion to Foucault*. London: Cambridge University Press, 115–140.

Davies, P. (2007) *Making a difference: working with users to develop research for policy and practice*. American Education Research Association Conference, Chicago, 9–13 April.

Delamont, S., Atkinson, P. & Parry, O. (2004) *Supervising the doctorate: a guide to success*. Maidenhead: Open University Press.

Delany, G. (2001) *Challenging knowledge: the university in the knowledge society*. Buckingham: Society for Research in Higher Education and Open University Press.

Derrida, J. (1982) *Margins of philosophy*, trans. Alan Bass. Chicago: University of Chicago Press.

Derrida, J. & Bass, A. (2001) *Writing and difference*. Chicago: Chicago University Press.

Donsbach, W. & Klett, B. (1993) Subjective objectivity: how journalists in four countries define a key term of their profession. *International Communication Gazette*, 51 (1), 53–83.

Doucet, A. & Mauthner, N.S. (2008) What can be known and how? Narrated subjects and the listening guide. *Qualitative Research*, 8 (3), 399–409.

Drake, P. (2006) *Working for learning: a case of mathematics for teaching*. University of Sussex.

—— (2009) Working for learning: teaching assistants developing mathematics for teaching. *Journal of Mathematics Teacher Education*, 12 (1), 67–82.

—— (2010) Grasping at methodological understanding: a cautionary tale from insider research. *International Journal of Research and Method in Education*, 33 (1), 85–99.

Drake, P. & Heath, L. (2008) Insider researchers in schools and universities: the case of the professional doctorate. In P. Sikes & T. Potts (eds), *Researching education from the inside: investigating institutions from within*. London: Routledge, 127–143.

Dunne, M. & Johnson, J. (1994) Research in gender and mathematics education: the production of difference. In P. Ernest (ed.), *Mathematics, education and philosophy*. London: Falmer Press, 221–229.

Dunne, M., Pryor, J. & Yates, P. (2005) *Becoming a researcher: a research companion for the social sciences*. Maidenhead: Open University Press.

Ebeid, A. (2008) Exploring the problems of hard to reach families and children-in-need and the support they received from their health visitors. Unpublished doctoral thesis, University of Sussex.

Edwards, R. & Miller, K. (2007) Putting the context into learning. *Pedagogy, Culture & Society*, 15 (3), 263–274.

Engeström, Y. (1996) Developmental work research as educational research. *Nordisk Pedagogik: Journal of Nordic Educational Research*, 16 (5), 131–143.

—— (2001) Expansive learning at work: toward an activity theoretical reconceptualization. *Journal of Education and Work*, 14 (1), 133–156.

Eraut, M. (1994) *Developing professional knowledge and competence*. London: Falmer Press.

—— (2003) Personal communication.

—— (2004a) Informal learning in the workplace. *Studies in Continuing Education*, 26 (2), 247–273.

—— (2004b) Practice based evidence. In G. Thomas & R. Pring (eds), *Evidence-based practice in education*. Maidenhead: Open University Press, 91–101.

—— (2007) Learning from other people in the workplace. *Oxford Review of Education*, 33 (4), 403–422.

Erben, M. (2002) Educative purpose and transdisciplinary compass in Auto/Biography: suicide and literature, cinema and collective subjectivities. *Auto/Biography*, X (1–2), 55–66.

ESRC (Economic and Social Research Council) (2009) Postgraduate training framework: a strategy for delivering excellence, online: www.esrcsocietytoday.ac.uk/ESRCInfoCentre/opportunities/postgraduate/fundingopportunities/ptf.aspx. Accessed 12 August 2009.

Finn, C. (1997) *Social reality*. London: Routledge.

Flyvbjerg, B. (2001) *Making social science matter: why social inquiry fails and how it can succeed again*. Cambridge: Cambridge University Press.

Foucault, M. (1977) *Discipline and punish*. London: Penguin.

Geertz, C. (1973) *The interpretation of cultures*. New York: Basic Books.

—— (2001, 6 July) Empowering Aristotle. *Science*, 293, 53.

Gergen, K.G. (2001) *Social constructivism in context*. London: Sage.

Gewirtz, S. & Ozga, J. (1994) Interviewing the education policy elite. In G. Walford (ed.), *Researching the powerful in education*. London: UCL Press, 186–203.

Gibbons, M., Limoges, C., Nowotny, H., Schwartzman, S., Scott, P. & Trow, M. (1994) *The new production of knowledge: the dynamics of science and research in contemporary societies*. London: Sage.

Giddens, A. (1977) Positivism and its critics. *Studies in Social and Political Theory*, 29–95.

Glaser, B.G. & Strauss, A.L. (1987) *The discovery of grounded theory: strategies for qualitative research*. Chicago: Aldine.

Goodson, I.F. (1992) Studying teachers' lives: problems and possibilities. In I.F. Goodson (ed.), *Studying teachers' lives*. London: Routledge, 234–249.

Gorman, S. (2007) Managing research ethics: a head-on collision? In A. Campbell & S. Groundwater-Smith (eds), *An ethical approach to practitioner research*. Abingdon: Routledge, 8–23.

Gramsci, A. (1971) *Selections from the prison notebooks of Antonio Gramsci*, trans. Quintin Hoare and G. Smith, New York: International Publishing.

Gregory, M. (1995) Implications of the introduction of the Doctor of Education degree in british universities: can the EdD reach parts the PhD cannot? *The Vocational Aspect of Education*, 47 (2), 177–188.

Griffiths, V., Thompson, S. & Hryniewicz, L. (2010) Developing a research profile: mentoring and support for teacher educators. *Professional Development in Education*, 36 (1), 245–262.

Guba, E.G. & Lincoln, Y.S. (1989) *Fourth generation evaluation*. London: Sage.

Gutierrez, K.D., Baquedano-López, P. & Tejada, C. (1999) Rethinking diversity: hybridity and hybrid language practices in the third space. *Mind, Culture, and Activity*, 6 (4), 286–303.

Gutting, G.E. (ed.) (1994) *The Cambridge companion to Foucault*, London: Cambridge University Press.

Hajer, M.A. (1995) *The politics of environmental discourse: ecological modernization and the policy process*. Wotton-under-Edge: Clarendon Press.

Hammersley, M. (1993) Educational research: current issues. *Open University study guide: educational research methods E824, Reader 1*. London: Paul Chapman Publishing and Open University Press.

Hammersley, M. & Atkinson, P. (1983) *Ethnography*. Cambridge: Tavistock.

—— (1995) *Ethnography*, 2nd edn. Cambridge: Tavistock.

Harding, S. (1986) *The science question in feminism*. Ithaca: Cornell University Press.

Hargreaves, D.H. (1999) Revitalising educational research: lessons from the past and proposals for the future. *Cambridge Journal of Education*, 29 (2), 239–249.

—— (2007) Teaching as a research-based profession: possibilities and prospects [Paper presented at the Teacher Training Agency Annual Lecture, London 1996]. In M. Hammersley (ed.), *Educational research and evidence-based practice*. London: Open University Press and Sage, 3–17.

Harms, D. (1979) *The Belmont report: ethical principles and guidelines for the protection of human subjects of research*. The National Commission for the Protection of Human Subjects of Biomedical and Behavioral Research, United States Department of Health, Education, and Welfare, online: www.hhs.gov/ohrp/humansubjects/guidance/belmont.htm. Accessed 13 May 2010.

Heath, L. (2005) Supervision of professional doctorates: education doctorates in English universities. Unpublished doctoral thesis, University of Brighton.

Heisenberg, W. (1927) Ueber den anschaulichen Inhalt der quantentheoretischen Kinematik unt Mechanik. *Zeitschrift für Physik*, 43, 172–198. English translation in J.A. Wheeler and W.H. Zurek (eds) (1983) *Quantum theory and measurement*. Princeton, NJ: Princeton University Press, 62–84.

Hellawell, D. (2006) Inside-out: analysis of the insider–outsider concept as a heuristic device to develop reflexivity in students doing qualitative research. *Teaching in Higher Education*, 11 (4), 483–494.

Hill, L., Gray, R., Stroud, J. & Chiripanyanga, S. (2009) Inter-professional learning to prepare medical and social work students for practice with refugees and asylum seekers. *Social Work Education: The International Journal*, 28 (3), 298–308.

Hillage, J., Pearson, R., Anderson, A. & Tamkin, P. (1998) *Excellence in research on schools*. London: DfEE.

Hockey, J. (1994) New territory: problems of adjusting to the first year of a social science PhD. *Studies in Higher Education*, 19 (2), 177–190.

Humphrey, C. (2007) Insider-outsider: activating the hyphen. *Action Research*, 5 (1), 11–26.

Hunt, C. & Sampson, F. (2006) *Writing: self and reflexivity*. Basingstoke: Palgrave Macmillan.

Ivanic, R. (1998) *Writing and identity: the discoursal construction of identity in academic writing*. Amsterdam and Philadelphia: John Benjamins Publishing Company.

Jacob, M. (2000) Mode 2 in context: the contract researcher, the university and the knowledge society. In M. Jacob & T. Hellestrom (eds), *The Future of Knowledge Production in the Academy*. Buckingham: Society for Research in Higher Education and Open University Press, 11–27.

Johnson, L., Lee, A. & Green, B. (2000) The PhD and the autonomous self: gender, rationality and postgraduate pedagogy. *Studies in Higher Education*, 25 (2), 135–147.

Kamler, B. & Thomson, P. (2008) The failure of dissertation advice books: toward alternative pedagogies for doctoral writing. *Educational Researcher*, 37 (8), 507–514.

Kelly, A. (1989) Education or indoctrination: the ethics of school-based action research. In R.G. Burgess (ed.), *The ethics of educational research*. Lewes: Falmer Press, 100–113.

Kuhn, T.S. (1970) *The structure of scientific revolutions*. Chicago: University of Chicago Press.

Labaree, R.V. (2002) The risk of 'going observationalist': negotiating the hidden dilemmas of being an insider participant observer. *Qualitative Research*, 2 (1), 97–122.

Lakoff, G. & Johnson, M. (1980) *Metaphors we live by*. Chicago: University of Chicago Press.

Lather, P. (1991) *Getting smart: feminist research and pedagogy with-in the postmodern*. New York: Routledge.

—— (1993) Fertile obsession: validity after poststructuralism. *Sociological Quarterly*, 34 (4), 673–693.

Lather, P. & Smithies, C. (1997) *Troubling the angels*. Boulder, CO: Westview Press.

Lave, J. (1988) *Cognition in practice: mind, mathematics and culture in everyday life*. Cambridge: Cambridge University Press.

Lave, J. & Wenger, E. (1991) *Situated learning: legitimate peripheral participation*. Cambridge: Cambridge University Press.

Lee, A., Green, B. & Brennan, M. (2000) Organisational knowledge, professional practice and the professional doctorate at work. In J. Garrick & R.C. (eds), *Research and knowledge at work: perspectives, case studies and innovative strategies*. London: Routledge, 117–136.

Leinhardt, G., Young, K.M. & Merriman, J. (1995) Integrating professional knowledge: the theory of practice and the practice of theory. *Learning and Instruction*, 5 (4), 401–408.

Leonard, D. (2001) *A woman's guide to doctoral studies*. Buckingham: Open University Press.

—— (2009) The doctorate in the life course. In P. Thomson & M. Walker (eds), *Doctoral supervisor's companion*. London: Routledge, 171–184.

Lincoln, Y.S. (1997) Self, subject, audience, text: living at the edge, writing in the margins. In W. Tierney & Y.S. Lincoln (eds), *Representation and the text: re-framing the narrative voice*. Albany: State University of New York Press, 37–56.

Lincoln, Y.S. & Guba, E.G. (1985) *Naturalistic inquiry*. Newbury Park, CA: Sage.

Lunt, I. (2002) Professional doctorates in education. Commissioned article for The Higher Education Academy Education Subject Centre, online: http://escalate.ac.uk/1712. Accessed 13 May 2010.

Macfarlane, B. (2008) *Researching with integrity: the ethics of academic enquiry*. Abingdon: Routledge.

MacLure, M. (1995) Theoretical resources. *Educational Action Research*, 3 (1), 106–116.

—— (2003) *Discourse in educational and social research*. Buckingham: Open University Press.

Macrae, S., Brown, M. & Rodd, M. (2003) *Students' experience of undergraduate mathematics*. Economic and Social Research Council, Report R000238564, online: www.esrcsocietytoday.ac.uk/ESRCInfoCentre. Accessed 13 May 2010.

Maher, D., Seaton, L., McMullen, C., Fitzgerald, T., Otsuji, E. & Lee, A. (2008) 'Becoming and being writers': the experiences of doctoral students in writing groups. *Studies in Continuing Education*, 30 (3), 263–275.

Malfroy, J. (2005) Doctoral supervision, workplace research and changing pedagogic practices. *Higher Education Research and Development*, 24 (2), 165–178.

Manathunga, C. (2002) *Research supervisor educational development: turning the light on private space*. Paper presented at the 4th World Conference of the International Consortium for Educational Development in Higher Education (ICED), Perth, Australia.

Maxwell, T. & Shanahan, P. (1997) Towards a reconceptualisation of the doctorate: issues arising from comparative data relating to the education doctorate degree in Australia. *Studies in Higher Education*, 22 (2), 133–150.

Maxwell, T., Shanahan, P. & Green, P. (2001) *Doctoral education and professional practice: the next generation?* Armidale, NSW: University of New England.

Mercer, J. (2007) The challenges of insider research in educational institutions: wielding a double-edged sword and resolving delicate dilemmas. *Oxford Review of Education*, 33 (1), 1–17.

Merton, R.K. & Storer, N.W. (1973) *The sociology of science*. Chicago: Chicago University Press.

Miles, M.B. & Huberman, A.M. (1994) *Qualitative data analysis: an expanded source book*, 2nd edn. Thousand Oaks, CA: Sage.

Milgram, S. (1974) *Obedience to authority: an experimental view*. New York: Harper Row.

Miller, N. (1993) Doing adult education research through autobiography. In N. Miller & D.J. Jones (eds), *Research Reflecting Practice*. Boston: SCUTREA, 88–92.

Moore, B. (2007) Original sin and insider research. *Action Research*, 5 (1), 27–39.

Murray, J. (2008) Teacher educators' induction into higher education: work-based learning in the micro communities of teacher education. *European Journal of Teacher Education*, 31 (2), 117–133.

Myers, K. (1996) Doctor Who. *Education* 187 (10), 9.

Neumann, R. (2005) Doctoral differences: professional doctorates and PhDs compared. *Journal of Higher Education Policy and Management*, 27 (2), 173–188.

Newkirk, T. (1996) Seduction and betrayal in qualitative research. In P. Mortensen & G.E. Kirsch (eds), *Ethics and representation in qualitative studies of literacy*. Urbana, IL: National Council of Teachers of English, 3–16.

Nightingale, D.J. & Cromby, J. (1999) *Social constructionist psychology: a critical analysis of theory and practice*. Buckingham: Open University Press.

Oakley, A., Strange, V., Toroyan, T., Wiggins, M., Roberts, I. & Stephenson, J. (2003) Using random allocation to evaluate social interventions: three recent U.K. examples. *Annals of the American Academy of Political and Social Science*, 589, 170–189.

OST (Office of Science and Technology) (1993) *Realising our potential: a strategy for science, engineering and technology*. London: HMSO.

Ozga, J. & Gewirtz, S. (1994) Sex, lies and audiotape: interviewing the education policy elite. In D. Halpin & B. Troyna (eds), *Researching education policy: ethical and methodological issues*. London and Washington: Falmer Press, 121–135.

Paechter, C. (1996) Power, knowledge and the confessional in qualitative research. *Discourse: studies in the Cultural Politics of Education*, 17 (1), 75–84.

Parker, I. (1997) Discursive psychology. In D. Fox & I. Prilleltensky (eds), *Critical psychology: an introduction*. London: Sage.

Peterson, C. & Seligman, M.E.P. (2004) *Character strengths and virtues: a handbook and classification*. New York: American Psychological Association and Oxford University Press.

Platt, J. (1981) On interviewing one's peers. *The British Journal of Sociology*, 32 (1), 75–91.

Polyani, M. (1966) *The tacit dimension*. New York: Doubleday.

Pryor, J. (2000) Hearing young children's voices in qualitative research: problems and possibilities. Unpublished, updated version of paper presented at European Conference on Educational Research, Bath, September 1995.

Pryor, J. & Crossouard, B. (2008) A socio-cultural theorisation of formative assessment. *Oxford Review of Education*, 34 (1), 1–20.

QAA (Qualifications and Assessment Authority) (2008, August) *The framework for higher education qualifications in England, Wales and Northern Ireland*, online: www.qaa.ac.uk/academicinfrastructure/FHEQ/EWNI08/default.asp. Accessed 21 May 2010.

Qin, J., Jurisica, I., Liddy, E.D., Jansen, B.J., Spink, A., Priss, U. & Norton, M.J. (2000) Working with data: discovering knowledge through mining and analysis; systematic knowledge management and knowledge discovery; text mining; methodological approach in discovering user search patterns through web log analysis; knowledge discovery in databases using formal concept analysis; knowledge discovery with a little perspective. *Bulletin of the American Society for Information Science*, 27 (1), 7–23.

Rosen, H. (1998) *Speaking from memory: the study of autobiographical discourses*. Oakhill: Trentham Books.

Saunders, L. (2007) Professional values and research values: from dilemmas to diversity. In A. Campbell & S. Groundwater-Smith (eds), *An ethical approach to practitioner research*. London and New York: Routledge, 62–74.

Schön, D. (1983) *The reflective practitioner*. San Francisco: Jossey-Bass.

—— (1987) *Educating the reflective practitioner*. San Francisco: Jossey-Bass.

Schostak, J.L. (2000) *Understanding, designing and conducting qualitative research in education: framing the project*. Maidenhead: Open University Press.

Scott, D., Brown, A., Lunt, I. & Thorne, L. (2004) *Professional doctorates: integrating professional and academic knowledge*. Maidenhead: Society for Research in Higher Education and Open University Press.

—— (2009) Specialised knowledge in UK professions. In D. Boud & A. Lee (eds), *Changing practices of doctoral education*. Abingdon: Routledge, 143–156.

Scott, P. (1995) *The meanings of mass higher education*. Buckingham: Society for Research in Higher Education and Open University Press.

Sebba, J. (2007) Enhancing impact on policy-making through increasing user engagement in research. In L. Saunders (ed.), *Educational research and policy-making: exploring the border country between research and policy*. London: Routledge, 127–143.

Seddon, T. (2001) What is doctoral in doctoral education? In B. Green, T. Maxwell & P. Shanahan (eds), *Doctoral education and professional practice: the next generation?* Armidale, NSW: Kardoorair Press, 303–336.

Sikes, P. & Potts, A. (eds) (2008) *Researching education from the inside: investigations from within*. London and New York: Routledge.

Simons, H. (ed.) (1980) *Towards a science of the singular: essays about case study in educational research and evaluation*. Norwich: Centre for Applied Research in Education, University of East Anglia.

Simons, H. & Usher, R. (2000) *Situated ethics in educational research*. London: RoutledgeFalmer.

Stacey, J. (1988) Can there be a feminist ethnography? *Women's Studies International Forum*, 11 (1), 21–27.

Stake, R.E. (1981) Interview with Robert E. Stake. *Educational Evaluation and Policy Analysis*, 3 (3), 91–94.

Stanley, L. (1993) The knowing because experiencing subject: narratives, lives and auto/biographies. *Women's Studies International Forum*, 16 (3), 205–216.

—— (1999) http://ourworld.compuserve.com/homepages/lizstanley. Accessed 2004.

Stronach, I. & MacLure, M. (1997) *Educational research undone: the postmodern embrace*. London: Open University Press.

Stuart, M. (1993) Speaking personally: the self in educational oral history work. In N. Miller & D.J. Jones (eds), *Research reflecting practice*. Boston: SCUTREA, 95–97.

Taylor, A. (2007) *Identifying good pedagogical practices in Doctorates of Education*. Paper presented at The Professional Doctorate seminar, Roehampton University, 5 December 2007.

Taylor, J. (2003) Institutional diversity in UK higher education: policy and outcomes since the end of the binary divide. *Higher Education Quarterly*, 57 (3), 266–293.

Thorne, L.E. (2001) Doctoral level learning: customization for communities of practice. In B. Green, T.W. Maxwell & P. Shanahan (eds), *Doctoral education and professional practice: the next generation*. Armidale, NSW: Kardoorair Press, 247–274.

Tierney, W. (1997) Lost in translation: time and voice in qualitative research. In W. Tierney & Y.S. Lincoln (eds), *Representation and the text: re-framing the narrative voice*. Albany: State University of New York Press, 23–38.

Tolbert, P.S. & Zucker, L.G. (1996) The institutionalization of institutional theory. In S.R. Clegg, C. Hardy & W.R. Nord (eds), *Handbook of organization studies*. London: Sage, 175–190.

Torrance, H. & Sebba, J. (2007) *Reviewing reviews: towards a better understanding of the role of research reviews*. Teaching and learning research programme research briefing, London.

UKCGE (2002) Professional doctorates. United Kingdom Council for Graduate Education, online: www.ukcge.ac.uk/Resources/UKCGE/Documents/PDF/Professional%20Doctorates%202002.pdf. Accessed 13 May 2010.

—— (2008) *The changing role of the supervisor*. United Kingdom Council for Graduate Education conference, University of Reading, 3 December 2008. www.ukcge.ac.uk/events/pastevents/0809area/supervisors08.htm.

—— (2009) *International conference on professional doctorates*. United Kingdom Council for Graduate Education conference, Middlesex University and UKCGE, 9–10 November 2009. www.ukcge.ac.uk/events/pastevents/0910area/icpd.

Usher, R. (2000) Imposing structure: enabling play – new knowledge production in the 'real world' university. In C. Symes & J. Mcintyre (eds), *Working knowledge: the new vocationalism and higher education*. Buckingham: Society for Research in Higher Education and Open University Press, 98–110.

van Heugten, K. (2004) Managing insider research: learning from experience. *Qualitative Social Work: Research and Practice*, 3 (2), 203–219.

Vygotsky, L.S. (1978) *Mind in society: the development of higher psychological processes*. Cambridge, MA: Harvard University Press.

Walford, G. (1998) Introduction: research accounts count. In G. Walford (ed.), *Doing research about education*. London and Philadelphia: Falmer Press, 1–10.

Webster, P. (2010) Codes of conduct. In M. Gray & S.A. Webb (eds), *Ethics and value perspectives in social work*. London: Palgrave, 31–40.

Wellington, J. & Sikes, P. (2006) A doctorate in a tight compartment: why students choose to do a professional doctorate and its impact on their personal and professional lives. *Studies in Higher Education*, 31 (6), 723–734.

Wenger, E. (1998) *Communities of practice: learning, meaning and identity*. Cambridge: Cambridge University Press.

West, L. & Alexopoulou, F. (1993) On keeping a diary: a new approach to reflexive practice. In N. Miller & D.J. Jones (eds), *Research reflecting practice*. Boston: SCUTREA, 104–106.

Whitehead, J. & McNiff, J. (2006) *Action research living theory*. London: Sage.

Zimbardo, P.G. (1971) *The power and pathology of imprisonment*. Congressional Record. First Session on Corrections, Part II, Prisons, Prison Reform and Prisoner's Rights: California. Subcommittee No. 3, of the Committee on the Judiciary. Washington, DC: U.S. Government Printing Office, Serial No. 15, 1971-10-25.

Zuber-Skerritt, O. & Ryan, Y. (1994) *Quality in postgraduate education*. London: Kogan Page.

Index